Once Upon a Doomed Trip

CONNY CONNORS

First Edition

NEWMAN SPRINGS PUBLISHING
320 Broad Street
Red Bank, NJ 07701

First originally published by Newman Springs Publishing 2023

ISBN 978-1-68498-913-3 (Paperback)
ISBN 978-1-68498-914-0 (Digital)

Printed in the United States of America

To my husband, Alex, many thanks for your patience while writing the book and telling me, "enough with the editing. Your story is very well laid **out**, I say this with not a speck of **doubt**."

To Eli, I dedicate this book to you, many thanks for all you've done to keep the ones you love happy, as well as all others.

While touring South America, some of the sites
in the amazing and unparalleled **Brazil**,
certainly gave my group the **chill**.

To the ones that asked me, "Conny, what
happened on this much-discussed trip?"
I always answered, "Yes, it really was off the **chart**."
That being said, I didn't know where to **start**.

One day, the idea popped, I'd write
the unbelievable **story**.
Finally, I did and found my **glory**.

Anyone who traveled, or in the midst of traveling,
perhaps planning a trip, yes **Indeed**,
This book is a must-**read**.

Anyone employed in the travel industry, prior
to your next group booking, consider a **break**,
read this book, before making a **mistake**.

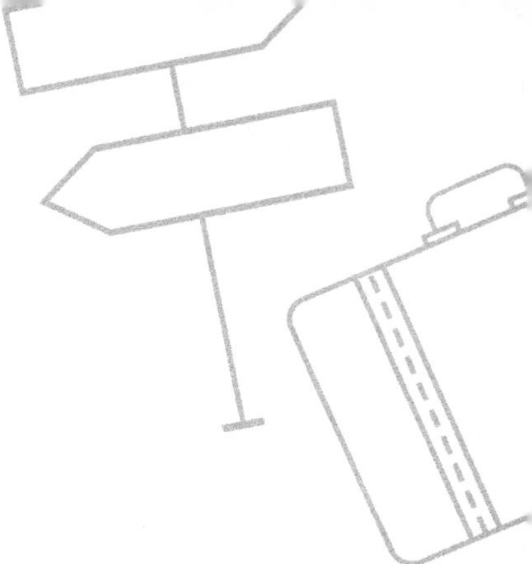

Anyone wishing to become a lawyer, perhaps
presently studying for that degree, or now
employed in the field of law, busy or **not**,
give this book a fair **shot**.

It's been subdued for a long, long **time**,
revealing the truth is not a **crime**.

What I'm about to expose, may not sit **well**,
however, this story has found its path to show and **tell**.

To an unbelievable journey of the good,
bad, ugly and much **more**,
the following true tale will open the **door**.

As you're reading, you'll probably crack a
smile, shed a tear, or learn something **new**,
and for some, it'll be a valuable **clue**.

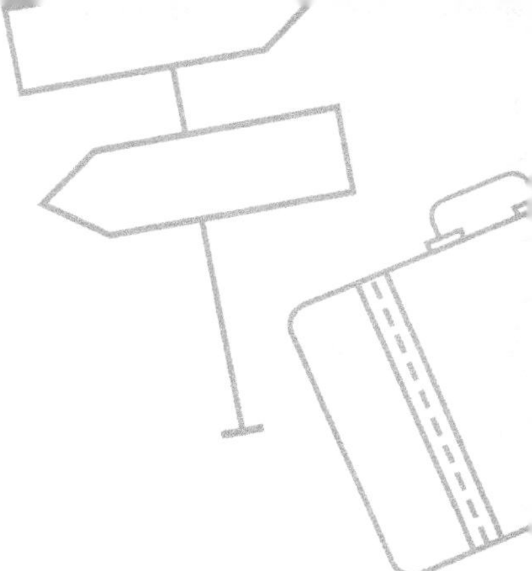

Part 1: The Planning of the Trip

Hopefully, another successful group
journey was in the planning **phase**,
little did I know, it was just a **phrase**.

Part 2: During the Trip

Plenty of ruined experiences came my **way**,
from the truth, the lousy guide ran **away**.

Part 3: Post Trip

As a result of many lies by my conniving
lawyer, an unfaithful money-**seeker**,
for sure, he proved to be the biggest **cheater**.
But not for **long**,
There was just too much **wrong**.

CONTENTS

Part 3: Post trip

AUTHOR'S NOTE

This book is a work of nonfiction. However, all names, locations, and identifying characteristics have been fictionalized. Those of real persons that have any resemblance to the fictionalized names, locations, and identifying characteristics are strictly coincidental. All statements and opinions in the book are my own.

Connyconnors1@gmail.com

PART 1

The Planning of the Trip

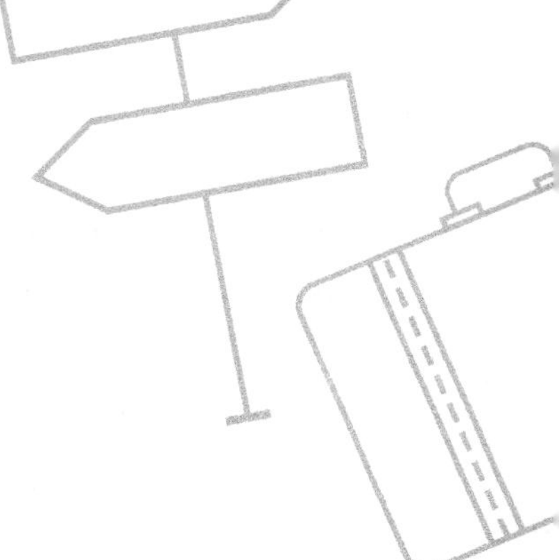

CHAPTER 1

In the Beginning

SINCE TRAVELING AND UNITING PEOPLE are two of my numerous passions, I tended to arrange group cruises every few years. Although travel agents don't necessarily accompany their groups, I always joined my arranged trips simply because in the event any unforeseen issues occurred, I'd be right there to patch up the situation no matter the cost or any other issues. So, in addition to being the agent, I was the trip's leader as well.

Note: this role is not to be confused with that of a tour guide. The task of actually guiding tours providing sightseeing and regional knowledge falls upon the local guides.

Some years ago, on the last day of a successful group sailing to Panama Canal and the Caribbean, Jane, a beautiful blonde lady (a new client), was extremely happy with my services.

As a result, she asked me, "Conny, would you look into a South American cruise for me and my husband? Maybe more couples would join us!"

I replied, "Of course, with pleasure." I was humbled by her request and the trust towards me.

Post the exciting Panama Canal trip, it didn't take me long to discover a fabulous cruise that had an amazing itinerary covering Argentina, Brazil, and Uruguay, commencing and terminating in Buenos Aires, Argentina. This sailing's special feature was a stop in Rio de Janeiro, Brazil, for three full days.

Such lengthy docking for a cruise ship is rare. The reason of the extended stay was the sailing coincided with Rio Carnival Parade.

Note: a top travel magazine once published an article that said, "Nobody throws a party quite like Brazil and there's no Brazilian party quite like Rio's Carnival Parade. It's the world's largest carnival celebration, attracting participants exceeding the better part of a million people for some five days of explosive, flamboyant, samba-shaking fun."

End of note.

Soon after, I did some more research and learned the following:

The festivities take place at Rio de Janeiro's world-famous Parade stadium called The Sambadrome Marques de Sapucai. This event has been performed in the latter part of February every year since 1723.

Due to the extremely hot and humid February summer days, it is an all-night jubilation. After sunset, the internationally renowned Parade comes to life with enormous lights, blasting music, and costumes that are extremely extravagant.

Some eight months prior to the newly selected cruise, and busy as a bee, I initiated a new group sailing. Slowly but surely, the list grew to approximately forty members who had signed up and paid the refundable deposit. My husband Alex and I were part of the new journey as well. At a later date, I would add an optional few-nights stay (pre-sailing) in Buenos Aires, thus giving the members who haven't been there a chance to venture into this exciting and roaring city.

I looked forward to a unique and desirable voyage on the horizon. Thus begins the true story of a doomed trip taken many moons ago.

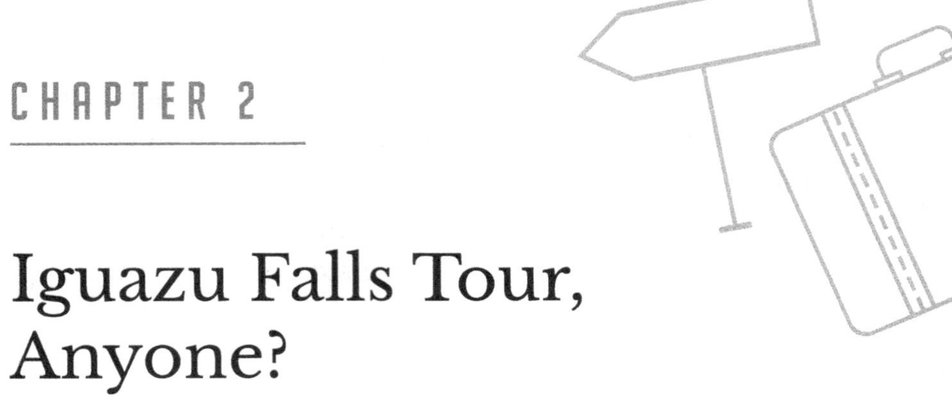

CHAPTER 2

Iguazu Falls Tour, Anyone?

A REFERRAL OF TWO NEW clients came to me highly recommended, Adele and her husband.

They booked the special cruise with joy and eagerly said, "Conny, since the sailing will commence in Buenos Aires and the Iguazu Falls are just a short flight away, please look for a two or three-day pre-cruise tour of the famous Falls."

I said, "Hooray for you! What a brilliant idea adding this natural wonder to our already-thrilling itinerary. I love when clients bring to my attention exciting and creative suggestions."

I further told her, "I'll get back to you as soon as I have all necessary information about your very sensible and certainly, logical request."

Note: the Iguazu Falls are some of the largest in the world. They're nestled between Argentina and Brazil, with a small portion in Paraguay. It would make a perfect add-on destination for my next group venturing South America.
End of Note.

Within a heartbeat, I started researching Adele's request. I gathered a list of experts for this worldly region and contacted them for a response. Within a timely manner, I received several calls back from various tour operators. After explaining the nature of my call, a three-day, two-night tour to Iguazu Falls, each offered a similar itinerary. However, the prices were more than I'd anticipated.

Before choosing one that I was most comfortable to work with, I received a fourth call from an agent based in New Jersey.

The man's first words were, "Hello, my name is Francisco, as in San Francisco."

I briefed him on my request and he replied, "I can arrange your visit to the beautiful Falls. I've been there 16 times in the last 16 years."

It didn't take long for him to share his background. He claimed the following:

- He'd been in the travel industry for many years as a tour guide and a travel agent.
- Expertise in Argentina, Uruguay, and Brazil.
- Apparently visiting each country often.
- The ability to speak multiple languages: English, Spanish, Portuguese, Hebrew, and some Yiddish
- Many references

Note: he made it very clear that in Brazil, he was only familiar with Rio de Janeiro (no other cities) and proudly stated that he'd been to 16 Rio Carnival Parades in the last 16 years.
End of Note.

Bingo! My group was mostly Hebrew/English-speaking members, so a guide who spoke a common minority language was an excellent ingredient for another successful trip.

For a start, I informed Francisco about the itinerary I'd be taking on a 13-night cruise around South America, commencing and concluding in Buenos Aires. I'd be needing:

- A one-night hotel stay in Buenos Aires
- A two or three day tour to the Iguazu Falls
- The best possible price

He listened intently and then answered, "I'll get back to you with a complete itinerary for a magnificent tour of the Falls."

As he promised, I received a call together with an email with the following proposal:

- A round-trip flight between Buenos Aires and Iguazu Falls
- Transfers between airports and hotels
- One-night stay at a city center hotel operated by a very nice family in Buenos Aires (tax and breakfast included)
- Two-night stay at a four-star hotel near the Falls (tax and breakfast included)
- Two and a half days touring the Argentinian and Brazilian side of the Falls
- A van with a driver
- A local English speaking private guide
- All entrance fees

- The price: $260 airfare plus $490 land arrangements totals $750 per person

Francisco said, "Because there is a flight involved, full payment is required after confirmation of the booking." He further stated, "I have a good friend working at the airline that your group will fly with, perhaps she can arrange for them to sit in prime seats on the flights."

I said, "Thank you for the prompt reply. You will hear from me if the deal is a go."

After comparing with the three other experts, I discovered that Francisco had the best prices for the same tour to the Falls. I also loved the fact that he spoke Hebrew, it would be an added feature on this special trip's itinerary.

The immediate full payment due in advance was not to my liking, but it was a small drawback to an otherwise wonderful package. The solution of early payment would be to strongly suggest the purchase of insurance exclusively for the pre-tour, which is normally ten percent of the tour's value. It's worth the peace of mind.

I then ran a background check on Francisco and his agency. After finding nothing negative, I emailed him, "Let's seal the deal! Give me some time to start a new file and reach out to my group."

Thereafter, I contacted Adele and sent her the exciting details of the Iguazu Falls tour.

I further said, "Look it over and review my proposal. There is no rush. We have plenty of time. Please bear in mind that full payment is required a few days after booking."

Her response was, "I'll review it and be in touch."

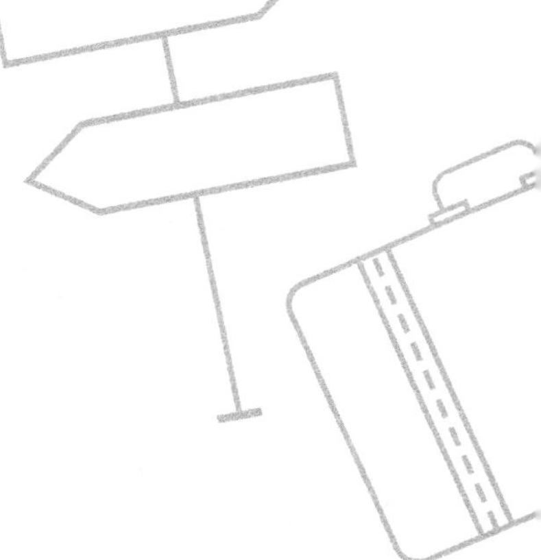

CHAPTER 3

Tours Galore

THE VERY NEXT DAY, I received another call from Francisco. I thought perhaps he'd taken an interest in the cruise's ports of call. He told me the following:

- "Please email me the ship's itinerary.
- If possible, also send me the ship's entire bus tour schedule for each port of call that they offer tours."

I was right. He had taken interest in the cruise's tours.

I fulfilled his request and the information was on its way to him.

He replied, "Many thanks, I'll get back to you with my suggestions and a proposal."

Perfect, I didn't mind options without commitment. I had never been to South America, so a good assistant was welcomed.

No sooner than later, Francisco emailed his recommendations regarding what to do and see after the Falls tour in Buenos Aires, also all ports of call during the cruise. We then went over the schedule.

1. Pre-cruise:
   a. Due to the group's varied flight arrival schedule, everyone would take taxis from the airport to the hotel on their own. The Argentine government regulates cab fares and rates are very reasonable.
   b. Reservations for three nights in Buenos Aires (same hotel prior to the Falls tour). The rate was very attractive including tax and breakfast. Since the price was unbeatable, the request for an early commitment would apply.
   c. Francisco would provide a private bus tour for the two full days in the blazing city of Buenos Aires and vicinity. Lunch not included.
   d. Transportation from the hotel to the pier for evening's set sail.
2. During the cruise's ports of call:
   a. Punta del Este, Uruguay: He'd arrange a full-day tour. Lunch included.
   b. Santos/São Paulo, Brazil: Francisco's friend/colleague, an expert in those two cities, would plan a one-day tour. Lunch not included.
   c. Rio de Janeiro, Brazil: He'd arrange a day and a half touring all of Rio's attractions. Lunch not included.

A very important purchase, tickets to Rio Carnival Parade. Francisco specifically said, "This could be tricky to maneuver. I'll provide your group with bleacher seating in section seven, which has the best view. A bus transfer to/from the parade and a parking spot at the stadium's lot. The rate will be $450 per person. This is an excellent price for an event that is in high demand, however, tickets are nonrefundable. In a pinch, reselling them is an option, should someone cancel. Please make this decision soon before the prices increase. Immediate purchase is essential in order to secure the $450 price. Conny, please tell everyone that the seating is merely space on concrete bleachers. Cushions are available to rent, but most of the time spectators stand during the performances on the flamboyant floats, followed by marching bands. Spectators will sit during clean-up of the flying debris from the floats. Anyone desiring better seats can purchase them. However, it will be more than double or even triple the price." Then he told me again that he'd been to 16 Rio Carnival Parades in the last 16 years.

d. Montevideo, Uruguay: Francisco would arrange a one-day tour. Lunch included.

3. Post cruise: Returning to Buenos Aires, the group members with morning flights would take taxis to the airport. The ones with night departures have the option to purchase a room for a half-day rate at the same hotel they'd stayed in before the cruise. In the evening, they'll head to the airport via taxis.

In the proposal, Francisco itemized the cost for each of his services to be prepaid and added the following information:

- All tour buses have air conditioning accommodating 40 passengers as well as a guide and driver.
- One exception, Santos/São Paulo, that bus would only have 30 seats.

- He actually sparked an idea saying, "If anyone from the ship's passengers would like to join your bus tours, you can make extra money for yourself." I put this suggestion on the back burner for later.

Francisco requested full payment (nonrefundable) due within a month.

I would be okay asking the tour members to prepay the Iguazu Falls tour, as well as the hotel stay in Buenos Aires for three nights and of course, Rio's Parade tickets. However, I was not comfortable enforcing full payment for the bus tours so far in advance. As a conscientious travel agent, I am a firm believer that people should have the freedom to do as they wish with their time and money. On top of that, I suspected that certain group members had already visited some of the ship's ports, so they'd most likely not join all of Francisco's tours. Furthermore, a few members might decline a bus tour, preferring to explore on their own.

I told Francisco, "Allow me a few days to think about the bus tours."

He replied, "Take your time, look it over, think about my plan, do your research, and perhaps compare my proposal with other agencies."

I thanked him, and said, "Shalom."

A deep breath came naturally. Francisco's seemingly endless suggestions were overwhelming. I needed time to digest his planning.

Over the next couple of days, I compared all of his services with other travel wholesalers and the ship's tour prices, his pricing was a bit lower for the same planning.

When I checked Rio Carnival Parade tickets with the cruise line, they were selling the exact same package for $650, that means $200 more than Francisco's price. It was a tedious undertaking. In the end, Francisco's proposal prevailed. I really loved the fact that he spoke Hebrew. Finding such a guide while having a mostly bilingual-speaking group (Hebrew and English) was an unlikely occurrence.

Regarding the payment for the bus tours, I'd honor Francisco's terms and prepay them. My plan was, throughout the cruise, I'd individually track each person's tours taken. On the last day of the cruise, which will be at sea, I'd settle everyone's account. To be fair and square, whatever I paid Francisco for each tour, I'd divide among the participants, adding only a small fee for my time and services. It would be a simple equation: the more members taking Francisco's tours, the less it would cost each individual.

I called him for the second time and said, "Let's seal the deal."

For my next project, I'd relay to the entire group all new additions to the trip.

They'd have exciting choices:

- Join the fabulous pre-cruise Iguazu Falls tour
- Sightsee in the blazing city of Buenos Aires (pre-cruise) for three nights
- Purchase Rio Carnival Parade tickets at a reasonably low rate for an event that is second to none
- Enjoy private bus tours at the cruise's major ports of call
- A half-day hotel stay (for those taking late flights back home)

I prepared all the options, prices, terms and conditions with full details and specific explanations. I correctly anticipated many questions (which soon came) and replied accordingly.

All understood the assessment and appreciated my flexibility. I always looked out for the comfort and welfare of each guest. That was my top priority.

As a result of this outreach, I was able to confirm prepayments for the Iguazu Falls tour, a three-night hotel stay in Buenos Aires, and Rio Carnival Parade tickets.

Slowly, I received each group member's desired options, along with the associated payments.

The planning of the trip was coming along very smoothly. From time to time, new tour members were added to my list. When I received their payments, I forwarded them to Francisco. The breakdown, thus far, was as follows:

- Approximately half of the group joined the Iguazu Falls tour
- All agreed to the Buenos Aires pre-cruise stay
- Everyone purchased Rio Carnival Parade tickets in advance
- Most of the members with night flights back home booked the hotel day rate

I was a happy agent looking forward to another successful trip. I'm allowed to dream.

CHAPTER 4

Unnecessary Information

During the months of trip planning, Francisco continuously revealed to me details about his personal life. We were communicating about travel services, and I felt things should remain on a professional level only. In an attempt of being polite, I lent him a listening ear to his stories, but I didn't take anything he said seriously.

Throughout these conversations, Francisco frequently brought to my attention that he had been to 16 Rio Carnival Parades in 16 years.

The sharing of his personal life did not cease. Francisco told me his age, marital status (single), living situation, and more.

Apparently, he had a lady friend who was very wealthy. I came to learn that she showed him great generosity and extended her wealth to him by providing hefty sums and items of great value. I did not understand Francisco's purpose in exposing such private and sensitive information. Whatever his reasons were, it was none of my business, however, I'd later find out what role that female friend really played in his personal and business encounters.

Though we were thousands of miles apart, I wanted to somehow meet him in person before the South American trip. A union almost happened when he was in Cancun and my schedule brought me to Cozumel at the same time. The two cities are not far apart, but our timing did not synchronize.

I finally met Francisco, when he traveled many miles visiting a city near my hometown, to partake in an LGBTQ pride Parade. He really liked street festivals. After all, it seemed that he'd told me more than 16 times that he had been to 16 Rio Carnival Parades in the last 16 years.

Now I could visualize who was on the other end during our phone conversations.

CHAPTER 5

An Interesting Request

One fine day, Francisco called, asking if it would be okay to give his new client my phone number as a reference. This seemed a bit strange that with the many references he claimed to have, I was the one he chose. We'd just barely begun working together, and he'd yet to show me any real results of his performance as a guide or otherwise. Why me? I didn't refuse his request, but I hoped no one would contact me.

I did receive a call from his new client. It was a lady, I asked her, "Did Francisco give you any other references?"

She replied, "No."

I thought this was even stranger. Little flags could be seen far on the horizon.

She then asked me about the quality of his services, and I replied, "Francisco and I started planning a group trip not long ago. Before hiring him, I checked his name and agency. Nothing negative popped up. So far, it's been smooth sailing, and I have no further data on him."

To date, I still wonder if she hired him. I regret not keeping her phone number on file.

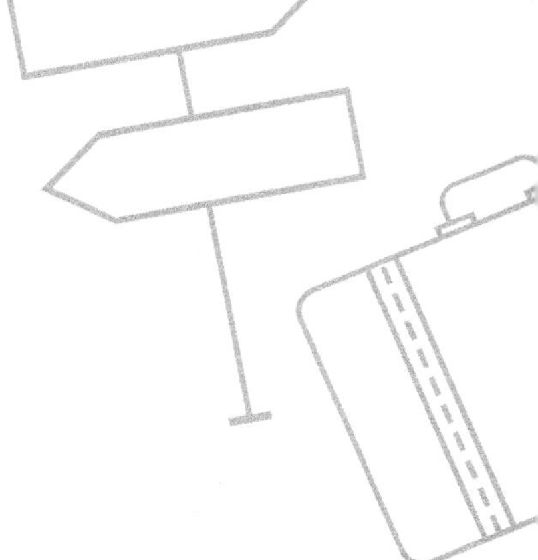

CHAPTER 6

Talking to a Wall

Many times throughout our planning, I reminded Francisco, "Please remember that practically half of the tour members are new clients. They signed up based on the fact that I was highly recommended due to my history of trying my best. The other half have traveled with me multiple times and knew me very well. I'm also aware that a few group participants do not have easy personalities. In fact, some of the ones I know are very good at being opinionated. However, impressing them is a goal you want to reach. Obviously, every member will be expecting their money's worth, and rightfully so."

My famous lines to Francisco were repeated over and again: "If you do a very good job, I look good. If you do a bad job, I look very bad. I hired you and every guest is relying on my best judgment, so please bring your top performance to the table. Do well, and there's a good chance it will result in more business for you. After all, travel is up the group's alley." In retrospect, I must have been talking to a wall.

I left him with one final note: "Just so you know, I am not revealing that we'll have a Hebrew-speaking guide. I'd like to keep it a surprise."

CHAPTER 7

Be Careful What You Say

I HEARD MANY TIMES FROM Francisco that he disliked Brazil and the Brazilians (with the exception of Rio de Janeiro). Doing business with them was not an option for him. Most of his comments on the country and its citizens were negative. Of course, he was entitled to his opinion, but keeping it to himself would have been smarter and on the diplomatic side. However, with the love that he showed for Rio de Janeiro and the famous Parade, Francisco could have been the lead spokesman or a promoter of that organization. After all, he constantly stressed that he'd been to 16 Rio Carnival Parades in 16 years.

If that was not enough, too many times for my ears, Francisco told me about two notorious subjects:

1. "Tell your clients that in Brazil, they should be very careful with money, jewelry, etc. Anything is subjected to theft."
2. "Rio Carnival Parade is managed by a mafia organization."

Listening to Francisco repeat those two alarming and disparaging statements over and again made me feel like I was brainwashed. Little flags were waving on the horizon.

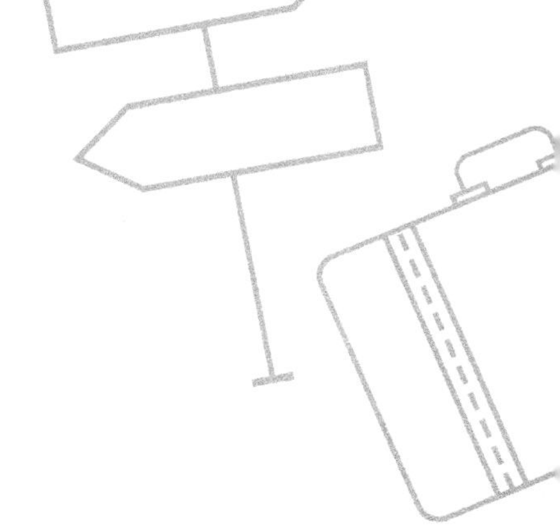

CHAPTER 8

Real *Real*

ONE SUNNY SUNDAY, FRANCISCO CALLED me while I was at a friend's house for brunch. Against my better judgment, I answered the phone on my day off. Couldn't he at least wait until Monday?

Francisco gave me the news that his bank charged him $1,000 due to the conversion fee from US dollars into Brazilian currency, which is called *real* (pronounced "ree-al").

This transaction was for the purchase of Rio Carnival Parade tickets. Needless to say, I was shocked. Even more so, he wanted me to pay the total fee (he's allowed to dream).

I told him, "Let's continue this issue on Monday."

My next conversation with him was the day after.

I said, "Can you provide me with proof from your bank regarding the $1,000?"

He replied, "Of course I can."

I never received any evidence to support his absurd story, and of course, I didn't give him a dime for his ludicrous request.

I eagerly wanted to cancel all of his bookings. However, at that time, he had received all the nonrefundable money.

What a horrible situation to be in. The little flags were starting to turn into big concerns. The only thing for me to do from here on—is watch him like a hawk.

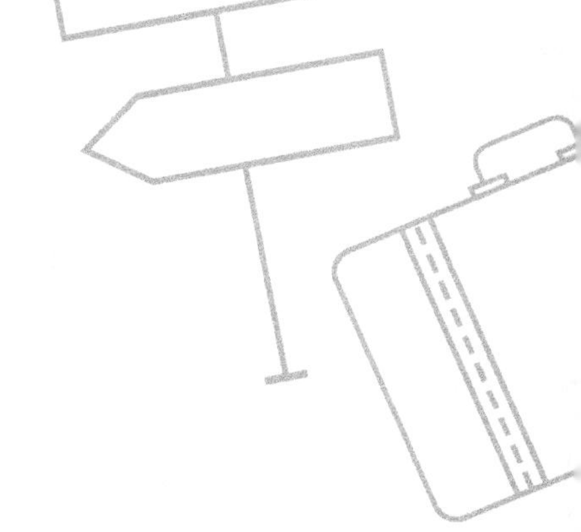

CHAPTER 9

Plus One

THE NEXT TIME FRANCISCO PHONED me, my heart started to race again. Now what?

His voice came over the phone, saying the following:

- I'm traveling with my good buddy to Buenos Aires.

Note: When Francisco had given me the name of the friend, I had the good sense to write his name in my important notes (in case I'd need to reference it later).
End of Note.

- Our plan is joining your group on the Falls tour, including the hotel stay in Buenos Aires the night before the pre-tour.
- We will help the private guide during the three days.
- After the Falls tour, I'll also lodge at the same hotel in Buenos Aires, and I'd be guiding the two tours during your stay in the city that's responsible for the tango.
- The day you'll board the ship, I'm flying to Punta del Este, Uruguay to visit my parents. The second

day of your cruise, the ship will dock there and I'll be guiding the tour in Punta del Este.

- The next port, my friend/colleague, Jose, will arrange a one-day tour to Santos/São Paulo. He is an expert in that region, and he'll provide an excellent guide.
- In Rio de Janeiro, Brazil, of course I'll be there guiding the one and a half days tour. The eve of Rio Carnival Parade, I'll provide a transfer to the Parade from the ship and back.
- Finally, Montevideo, Uruguay, my cousin will provide the day tour. She is a local and knowledgeable guide."

I didn't know if I should be happy, sad, or more frustrated. Oh well, it was no worse than the attempt of the $1,000 heist. Feeling somewhat in limbo, I tried to digest his plans.

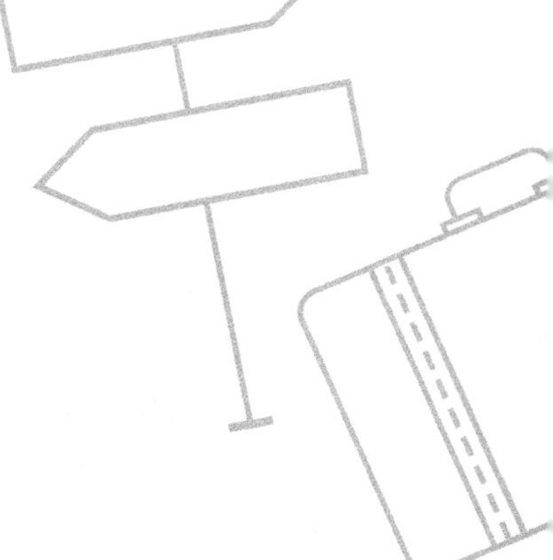

CHAPTER 10

One Third Fewer

Unfortunately, due to health issues and other circumstances worldwide, 13 group members canceled the trip, but thankfully, none of them carried any financial burden because…

1. The cruise deposit would be fully refunded once I released their cabins.
2. The hotel in Buenos Aires also provided a full refund.
3. Iguazu Falls was not refundable. However, due to my insistence that everyone purchase insurance specifically for this tour, full compensation will be granted.
4. Regarding Rio Carnival Parade's tickets, they are considered just like any other concert worldwide: nonrefundable. In the event of a cancelation, I promised that I'd try my best to resell them.

The fact remains that it was outside my call of duty. The service fee for my time and effort processing the 13 refunds was $25 per person. Almost everyone who canceled paid the small assessment (some even thought I should impose a higher amount).

The only person who disagreed and refused to pay was Adele. During the planning thus far, I had already experienced her character, a petty attitude and very short tempered. I didn't need nor desire any hardship from the prima donna for the 20 days in South America. So, good riddance to her.

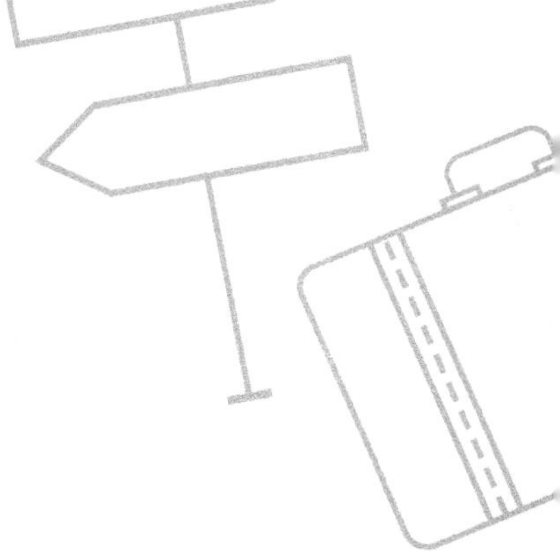

CHAPTER 11

Striking Gold

BECAUSE OF SOME ARROWS WHICH seemed to point towards unfaithful business practices from Francisco, I was in search of a way to check or track his work. Since most of the arrangements he'd made thus far, had taken place outside US borders, language barriers could come into play. My options were limited, however, being in a state of heightened suspicion, I'd have to be patient and wait for an opportunity to cross his unethical practice.

Within a short time, an idea popped into my hesitant mind, it pointed to the eight passengers (four couples) that booked and later canceled the Iguazu Falls tour, they paid $750 plus insurance which was paid to the insurance company. Fortunately, their cancelation gave me a clue: My first step was—to contact the airline and re-confirm the downsized group, making sure that the remaining members' names had correct spelling and ticket numbers.

While proceeding, shockingly I did not recognize the name on one of the tickets, that was fishy. I dashed to my file where I stored Francisco's friend's name. Lo and behold, yup! It was his buddy's name. The name change on the ticket is absolutely against airline policy, though I suppose not in Francisco's world. This type of tampering can be done by an insider that would take a chance to do something not allowed. Since Francisco told me he had a friend working at that particular airline, perhaps that person had taken a chance and illegally changed the name, probably for a fee.

Without a moment's hesitation, I placed a call to Francisco, planning to confront him about the wrongful name change.

He answered on the second ring, and I said, "Please, allow me a word or two. After the four couples canceled their trip to the Falls, I double-checked the reservation with the airline, and discovered that your friend's name was on one of my canceled tour member's ticket. Did your friend, the one who works for the airline, help you beat the no-name-change policy?"

To my surprise, Francisco did not deny my allegation. He just muttered some response about a switch here and a switch there.

The conversation went on, not making an ounce of sense, but spewing lots of nonsense. For the love of God, I could not get a straight answer from him. Being caught red-handed was probably embarrassing and upsetting. Trying to form an excuse on the spot, was not in the cards for Francisco.

Arguing would result in negative back-and-forth, so asking more questions would surely lead to more lies. I knew better than to continue this matter with a liar. It seemed as if watching Francisco like a hawk would help, but not solve any problems. I'm most likely dealing with a con artist. He already had all my non-refundable payments, so canceling his services was not an option.

The seven other air tickets were at Francisco's mercy and possibly in conjunction with his friend, that works at that particular airline. I decided not to ask whether he had plans for the remaining air tickets. He wouldn't have told me the truth anyway, so why ask.

Worries with this Hebrew speaking guide did not cease and my thoughts regarding the illegal name change was a potential problem. My only choice was—if indeed I'd have to handle this issue, I would deal with it at that time.

A reminder: The group members that elected to join the pre cruise tour to the Iguazu Falls prepaid $750 per person to Francisco. The breakdown was:

1. Airfare: $260 per person, a short round trip to the Falls from Buenos Aires. This amount had to be paid the same time as the booking was created, Francisco purchased the tickets accordingly.
2. Land arrangement: $490 per person, it consisted of hotel, private local guide, van/driver, and entrance fees to the Falls in Argentina and Brazil. These bookings did not require full payment (only a small deposit). Francisco paid accordingly. Full payment was due closer to the trip, which was months away.

How had Francisco struck gold in no time and effort?

The four couples that cancelled their entire trip, were totally reimbursed by the insurance company. My insistence of purchasing insurance defiantly paid off.

Months later the time came to pay the land arrangements. Of course, it was paid accordingly, but not for the eight people who cancelled. So, what happened to the $490x8? Only Francisco and I knew where it landed, in no time and effort.

My strong opinion: The insurance company should have contacted Francisco, or his agency, demanding a full review of all the money that was dispersed on the Iguazu Falls tour, and releasing the eight airline tickets to them.

CHAPTER 12

A Surprise in Store

THIS CHAPTER WILL BACKTRACK TO the trip's planning phase. It will depict two couples from the Midwest. They were Pete and Kiti, together with their best friends Shlomo and Sharon.

Regarding Pete, I had known him quite a few years. To me, he was always incredible and seemed to be quite a mensch ("nice person" in Yiddish). His good character held up throughout our friendship. However, his wife didn't equate to her husband's pleasant personality.

Regarding Shlomo and Sharon, I didn't know much about them, but Shlomo bore a reputation for having a stern temperament. It was also well-known that people appeared to orbit around this couple, hoping to score invitations to their lavish parties.

Both couples signed up for the cruise and the three-day stay in Buenos Aires (not the Falls tour).

When the third of the group canceled, Shlomo and Sharon were part of the downsizing. Kiti and Pete elected to remain with their travel plans, but they were rather sad about losing their best friend's company on a fabulous trip's itinerary. Kiti took it much harder than her husband, and I truly felt her disappointment.

Being an alert and conscientious travel agent, I checked daily for price drops on the ship's cabins. If indeed they had dropped, it would be my responsibility to contact the cruise line, as they are the only ones who can adjust and lock in the new lower rate. Indeed, fares did go down a couple of times.

When I informed the group members about the great savings, they were all thrilled about the hundreds of dollars back to their pockets. Coincidentally, I found one interior cabin on the second level at a price that couldn't be beat, thinking it might be useful at a later date for a new booking, I grabbed it in a heartbeat before someone else would snatch the fabulous deal.

Kiti's big disappointment about Shlomo and Sharon's cancellation was still very much on my mind.

I started to devise a plan that could make four people very happy by bringing Kiti's friends back on the fabulous cruise (possibly the Iguazu Falls tour as well).

My idea was, instead of charging Shlomo and Sharon full price, I'll reduce my earnings from the three days Fall tour (if indeed they'd book it) and the low-priced cabin on the fabulous cruise itinerary, should entice them to rebook. Wow! it's practically a two for one deal, however there is a condition: Since people at large gravitate to this couple's parties, I'd make Shlomo a silent pied piper. In hopes of adding newcomers to the trip.

Once I contacted them, both were surprised to hear from me. After informing the couple in full details regarding the new changes, they seemed eager and interested to rejoin.

Their feedback was, “Conny, your updated presentation is very intriguing.”

I said, “Think it over and please get back to me as soon as possible because I cannot hold the cabin for too long without commitment.”

The next morning, my first call was from Shlomo, he said, “It’s a go, oh, by the way, let’s surprise Pete and Kiti. A happy reunion will ensue.”

I agreed. We kept it hush-hush, and a second surprise was added to the trip.

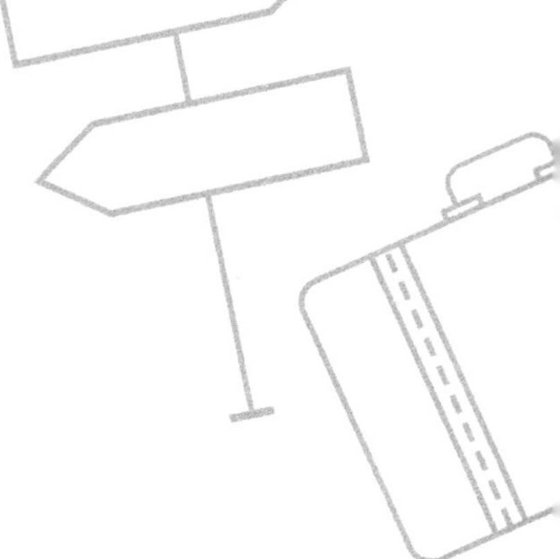

CHAPTER 13

Who Is Who?

THE FINAL HEADCOUNT—26 TOUR MEMBERS. 11 couples and four ladies would form my latest travel group. The attendees came from four corners of the world: United States, Canada, Mexico, and the United Kingdom. All group participants were instructed to arrange their own roundtrip airline tickets to Buenos Aires, Argentina.

Note: Out of the 26 tour members, 21 were English/ Hebrew speaking.

Only 14 group members took the opportunity to add on the three-day tour to the Iguazu Falls. They were as follows:

- Hellen
- Matilda
- Sally
- Conny (my husband, Alex, did not join the Iguazu Falls tour)
- Shlomo (aka the dictator) and Sharon
- Mr. and Mrs. Coban (scheduled for a private Falls tour)

Note: All of the above were arriving from the Midwestern region of the United States, and most knew each other.

- Mr. Goldfinger (Kiti's uncle) and his new wife (from Vancouver, Canada)
- Sam and Samantha (from Vancouver, Canada)
- Jack and Jacqueline (lived in Canada during the summer, and Arizona throughout the winter)

Note: The three couples above were close friends.

The remaining 12 tour members were not taking the Iguazu Falls tour. They were as follows:

- Mr. and Mrs. Kay
- Solomon and Sue
- Pete and Kiti
- Ruth, my stepmom
- My husband, Alex

Note: All of the above were from the Midwestern Region and some knew each other.

- Marty and Miriam from Mexico
- Nate and Nancy from the United Kingdom

Note: The two couples above (from Mexico and the UK) were completely new to the entire group, but it did not take long for them to mingle in.

CHAPTER 14

Up, Up, and Away

Sunday, February 8, En Route

Nearly eight months of planning, and the day to depart had finally arrived. Four of us—Matilda, Hellen, wonderful Sally, and I—boarded the flight to New York (where we would then connect to Buenos Aires). For the first time ever, I used mileage and upgraded my ticket to a first-class seat.

Upon arrival at JFK, our waiting time was approximately 90 minutes. The three ladies elected to browse and shop, while I preferred to sit and work on my needlepoint. It was a canvas of 32x22 inches and near completion. I hoped to finish it on the trip, if time allowed. Thus far, hundreds of hours had been invested in it, stitch by stitch. Since Alex and I are moving to a bigger home after the trip, I can finally set my canvas on the perfect wall in the new living room.

When needing to visit the ladies' room, I spotted Hellen and asked her to please watch my two little bags which contained very important documents and cash, she agreed. Returning several minutes later, I shockingly discovered that she was nowhere to be seen—unbelievable and so unreliable. Never again will I rely on her. Luckily, everything was intact and no one had spotted my belongings, not even security. I was in shock at her casual abandonment of my belongings.

However, what Hellen had just done was nothing in comparison to her careless and demeaning actions during the trip and thereafter.

We boarded the aircraft for the ten-hour journey to Buenos Aires. My seat was so remarkably comfortable that I wanted to share this wonderful experience with the others, so I went back to the ladies and asked if any of them wished to sit in first class for a while. The only one to take my offer was the irresponsible Hellen. She didn't even have the manners to say a word of appreciation.

A few hours into the flight, sleep was essential. My seat reclined 180 degrees, turning into a bed.

While snoozing, I'll share some of my humble tasks as a tour leader, while accompanying any group, I take pride in providing unique, specialized services to all of my travelers. The special attention included:

- In the event that a special occasion took place during the trip, such as birthdays, anniversaries, or alike, I made sure to bring the appropriate cards, modest gifts, and decorations with assorted themes.
- Ensuring that everyone had my cabin or room phone number. I availed myself, 24/7, to solve any problems, and answer all questions.
- Being a frequent cruiser, I was often invited to cocktail parties and special events. I'd typically request that my group be invited as well, so they could

enjoy the theme of the gathering, hors d'oeuvres and drinks. My requests were always granted.

- Helping the ladies get ready in the evenings. I'm quite handy with hair, so I told the women I'd gladly help if desired.
- Offering my long-distance minutes. Phone calls tend to be very expensive. Anytime I was able to gain a reliable signal, I would offer to share my limited minutes.
- Observing Shabbat Eve. As most of my clientele tended to be Jewish, I always made sure that the ship had necessary Friday night amenities. Those evenings gave a special meaning to my travelers.

Going beyond the call of duty was my pleasure.

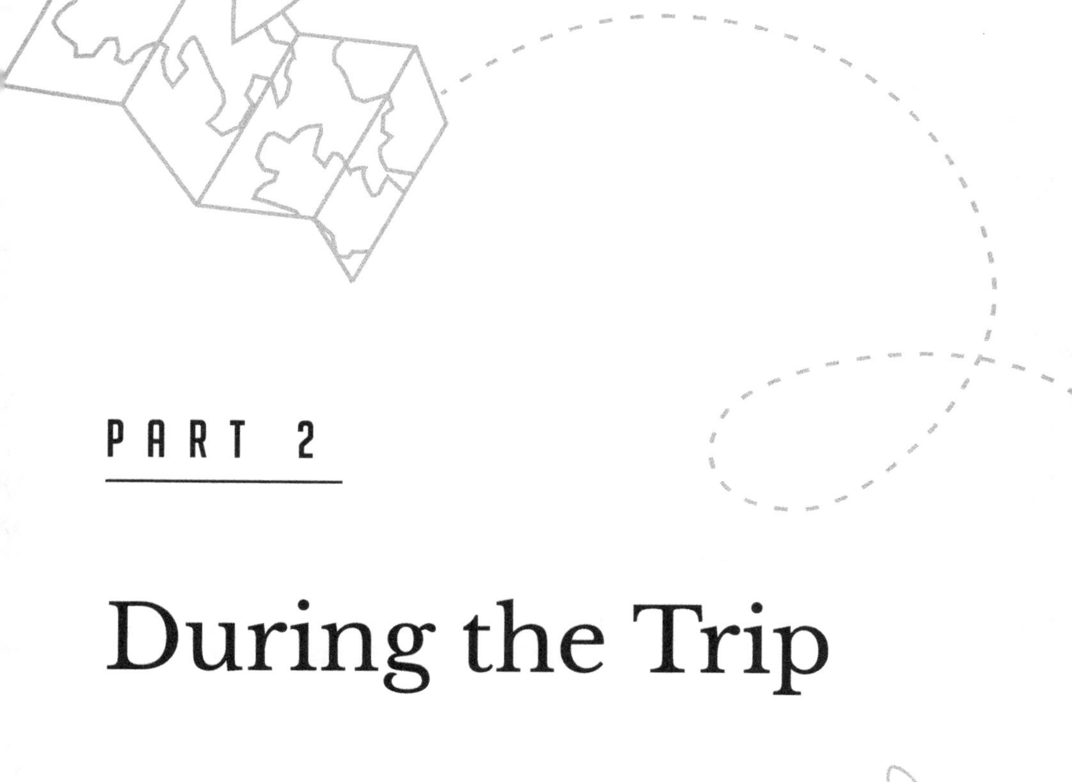

PART 2

During the Trip

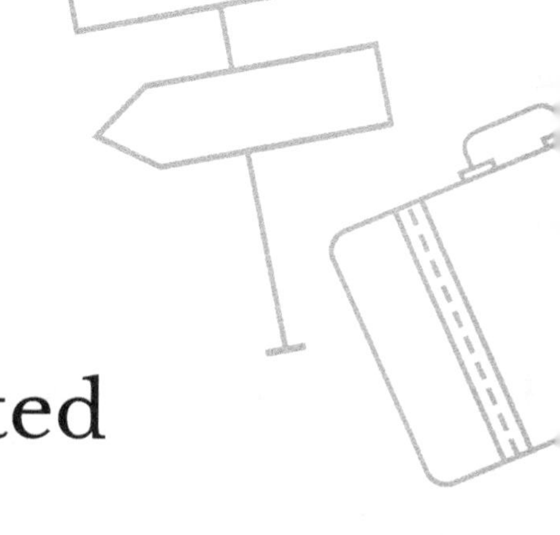

CHAPTER 15

The Long-Awaited Landing

Monday, February 9, Buenos Aires, Argentina

The flight from North America to South America was nothing short of wonderful. I slept until we landed. Thank goodness for the mileage program, enabling me to arrive rested and ready for the exciting adventures.

The four of us shared a taxi to the hotel. We arrived before noon. The front desk clerk was very kind, allowing us to check into our rooms early. I roomed with Matilda, and Sally with Hellen. The three ladies wanted to get some sleep. I was wide awake, and elected to walk around on a solo basis to familiarize myself with this tango-inspired city.

During the late afternoon, all of the trip members taking the Falls tour arrived. They were:

Mr. and Mrs. Goldfinger, Jack and Jacqueline, as well as Sam and Samantha.

Those three couples were all good friends. The last couple to arrive was, Shlomo and Sharon.

In the late afternoon, we all congregated in the hotel lobby. Francisco was scheduled to show up any minute. My excitement brewed because I was about to surprise the Falls tour group, with a Hebrew-speaking guide. No sooner than later, he arrived and greeted us in our common language. All the members were surprised and impressed. I prayed for no nonsense from the person whom I had very little trust.

After the pleasantries, we all went to dinner. Walking to a nearby restaurant was a good introduction to the city. The meal was okay but not much on the menu, except meat. That meant a little selection for me because when traveling, I generally stick to grains, vegetables, and fruits, so a hearty soup and a baked potato would be the safest for me. I noticed that Hellen and Francisco were splitting dinner which was a little strange.

Once we finished our meals, all of us stayed a while longer to further get acquainted with each other.

Oddly, Hellen took Francisco outside for a private conversation. No one asked or cared why. There was already an unusual pattern of behavior from this weird woman and unpredictable man. (What a combination) Soon after the two returned, we started our little walk back to the hotel.

While walking, Francisco put his arm around my shoulders. No threat; he's young enough to be my son. He seemed nervous and was repeating himself quite a bit.

Without me asking him what happened, he quietly said, "Hellen wanted me to give her $20 because she didn't have enough food." Strange was turning into a stranger situation. He continued: "She specifically told me, please don't tell anyone about this issue."

The fool gave Hellen the amount she'd requested. Frankly, I didn't want to have anything to do with this unusual situation. For the rest of the trip, Francisco couldn't stand the sight of her (I certainly agreed with him about that). However, he was totally wrong for exposing an issue that was supposed to be confidential between him and the strange Hellen.

It was getting rather late by the time we arrived at our rooms. The day had been very busy, and we all arrived after long flights from our homes. None of us were youngsters, so a good night's sleep was necessary.

Before retiring for the night, I had a small mission to accomplish, I told Matilda, "Sam has a birthday tomorrow. I'm going to wait awhile, then quickly and quietly decorate the exterior side of his room's door with two balloons and a 'Happy Birthday' sign. The humble gift, birthday cake, and a card, to be signed by all tour members, will be presented to him, the next day after dinner at the Falls."

Matilda said, "Oh, how nice! Shall I come along and help you decorate?"

I responded, "Surely! Four hands are better than two."

Our mission was soon accomplished, so we went to our room. After all, tomorrow will be another full day with lots of activities.

CHAPTER 16

Finally, the Iguazu Falls Tour

Tuesday, February 10, Buenos Aires, and Iguazu Falls (on the Argentinian side)

At breakfast, when the first eye contact between me and Sam occurred, I was anticipating some kind of acknowledgment regarding his festively decorated room door. I smiled, but no appreciation came my way. Oh well, maybe after dinner at the Falls, a birthday cake, humble gift, and a card signed by everyone would be appreciated, perhaps he'd show his gratitude at that time.

I noticed that Hellen and Sharon were preparing to-go sandwiches from the breakfast bar. This was not okay with me, especially at a mom-and-pop operation. I said nothing hoping it was a one-time deal.

Our flight to the Falls was scheduled for 3:00p.m., so we had the entire morning to ourselves and could do as we wished. Francisco announced that he had some errands to run, and if anyone wanted something, now was the time to ask. Only Matilda took his offer.

Some of us took a walk and others browsed at the local shops. Spotting a cute pair of high-heeled sandals was a good enough reason to make a purchase and add it to my shoe collection. I'm fairly petite, so adding height is always welcome at any given continent. Soon we returned to the hotel.

While I was gathering my overnight bag, Matilda entered the room all hyped up and irritated.

She said, "I don't like him, and I do not trust him."

My surprised response: "Who and what are you talking about?"

She went on, "Francisco told me that I owe him $20 for the two little items, but he didn't provide any receipts."

I thought, less than 24 hours has passed, and this is the second issue with him and a $20 bill. Some coincidence. I then told her, go and ask him pointedly for the receipts. I'm not sure if she did, but Matilda stayed miserable regarding this situation for what seemed to be the rest of Francisco's time with us. It was easy for her to do that.

What was the chance of another money issue of the same amount within less than a day?

Maybe Francisco wanted to recover the money that Hellen had demanded from him the night before (just a silly thought). I hoped that those two incidents would be the only ones. Wishful thinking.

We were all excited to finally start the Falls visit. The front desk clerk gave us some storage area for our excess belongings because we would be returning to the hotel for three additional nights after the Falls tour. The 14 of us congregated in the lobby, waiting for the transfer to the domestic airport. Upon arrival, I learned that our flight was delayed by an hour. I didn't mind, my needlepoint kept me busy and productive.

Finally, we boarded the aircraft. Shortly after reaching altitude, Francisco announced, loud and clear, "The captain planned a route directly over the Iguazu Falls especially for our group."

As Francisco finished his announcement, Shlomo dashed to my seat, extremely stressed and angry, he said, "Conny, did you know that the guide you hired is a liar?"

I thought, "Welcome to my world."

I asked him "What happened?"

He further said, "I know about aviation, no pilot in the world would ever change their flight pattern for anybody or anything, how and why did Francisco say that the pilot was flying over the Falls just for our group? That's a lie!"

Shlomo didn't tell me anything that I didn't already know. Instantly, I got my first headache of the trip.

From an aerial view, the formation of the Falls were spectacular.

The adjoined countries sharing the falling waters were:

- Argentina, with the biggest waterfall, called Devil's Throat
- Brazil, with stunning and many smaller clusters of Falls
- Paraguay, fewer Falls. Most people do not visit there since the other two are by far more tourist worthy

Shortly after landing, my headache unfortunately escalated. The local guide Marco met us and helped gather our belongings. He was nice and friendly from the very first moment. We then proceeded to the van that would be at our disposal for the entire tour. I truly wished, hoped, and prayed that I'd have zero problems on the Falls tour. By now, a little over 24 hours into the trip, I was seeing an obvious pattern of issues involving Francisco's problems with three different tour members Hellen, Matilda, and now Shlomo.

While driving to the hotel, our friendly guide briefed us on the surroundings. After checking in, we were allotted time to rest or roam around the property. We then reunited for a two-hour tour followed by dinner. Weatherwise, it was very hot and humid. The ones from the Midwest were not used to the high humidity, but we'd deal with the uncomfortable elements to view a natural Wonder of the World.

During the ride, Francisco took the liberty and the microphone to inform the group how diligently I had worked to put this trip together. At first, I thought, how nice of him to endorse my trip planning. However, his endorsements soon turned into unnecessary and unprofessional compliments that made me feel uncomfortable. Noticing that the vibers (older talkative Jewish women) were getting tired of Francisco's repetitive kind words towards me—and from time to time, they'd whisper into each other's ears—I had no choice but signal the guide to stop. Assuming jealously would get the vibers nowhere, but I still feared that the group at large was getting the wrong message.

Marco took us to the fascinating overlook. It was the portion of the South American continent where all three countries border each other. Argentina, Brazil, and Paraguay all touched each other, how interesting. Thereafter, we went to a restaurant for dinner.

Just like yesterday's meal, the selection of non-meat options was very limited. Oh well, a baked potato and some steamed veggies would be good enough for Conny. I noticed that Francisco consumed a lot of meat—this time, without sharing it.

After dinner, Sam's cake was served for dessert. The signed card and gift were given to him, thus his celebration continued on. I was surprised when still no expression of thanks was delivered. He didn't seem to know two words "thank you" or one-word "toda" ("thank you" in Hebrew).

While driving back to our hotel, Francisco took over the van's microphone again, he announced, "Look to your right and see the most lavish hotel in the Falls area, it's the one with a casino. As soon as the driver drops us off, he's done for the day. So, at approximately 9:00p.m., I'm taking a taxi to the casino. Anyone interested in joining me?"

I showed interest, but no one else did at that time.

After dinner, we sat out by the pool, enjoying the lovely evening breeze and reminiscing about the day's activities. Francisco came and said, "I am calling a taxi. Who's coming with me?"

Noticing that still no one else was interested, I told him, "Sorry, Francisco. I'm tired. I won't be joining you."

Truthfully, that's all I needed, one on one time with Francisco in a hotel's casino, at night, while the unnecessary compliments went on during the day. Food for the hungry vibers, was not to be offered by me.

The time to retire for the night was approaching. It had been a long day, complete with mostly good and a little not so good.

CHAPTER 17

No Wonder They Call It a World Wonder

Wednesday, February 11, Iguazu Falls, Argentina

Waking up the first morning at Iguazu Falls, I glanced outside my window to see the exotic flowers, and flourishing plants. Such a gorgeous garden captured my attention. It provided lovely scenery at sunrise.

I hoped that everyone had experienced a good night's sleep, however, no such luck. At breakfast, when I first looked at Sally, I was shocked by her appearance. The poor lady appeared as though she hadn't slept all night while carrying the world on her shoulders.

I asked, "What happened?"

She answered, "I couldn't sleep all night long. Hellen had the air conditioner blasting, and I was freezing."

I further asked, "Why didn't you tell her to raise the temperature?"

Sally responded, "Hellen was too hot and refused to touch the thermostat."

I couldn't believe it. At this point, I was so fed up with Hellen's selfishness by not thinking of her roommate's well-being. She'd allowed Sally to be cold and sleepless.

Feeling bad for her, my reply was, "I'll remedy the problem." The only choice is switching rooms. Sally will share a room with Matilda, and I'd spend the night with the ice queen. I certainly wasn't looking forward to that sweet treat.

After our morning meal, we gathered in the lobby for today's sightseeing at the Falls. Marco and the van driver were waiting to take us on the much-anticipated tour.

Upon arrival at the national park, the van had to be parked in the designated visitors' lot. We then took the park's train to the end of the tracks. Due to the mountain's formation, there was no other transportation to the Falls from this point on. The group would have to complete the final walk on foot.

Jacqueline preferred remaining at the starting point because she didn't want the risk of the hike, due to health issues. I felt sorry that she would wait with the driver, probably for a good several hours. Jack, her husband, announced he'd be joining the group, seemingly without caring that his wife missed a world attraction. What a shame. This trip was not for everyone.

We were on our way to start the walk towards the main Fall, known as Devil's Throat. The only possible path was a narrow, man-made pedestrian bridge stretching some 1,500 yards with railings on both sides. Being somewhat daredevilish (and a lifelong power walker), this type of venture is up my alley.

I asked Marco if it was safe to speed walk alone to the end of the bridge, he said, "Go for it, you cannot get lost."

So, while the rest were under the care of Francisco, his friend, and Marco, I felt comfortable walking faster and ahead of the group.

Proceeding on, there were some sharp turns, and at times, it seemed like air walking alongside a cliff (a bit scary for first timers). Nevertheless, the sky-high stroll was well worth the effort of every step along Mother Nature's geological creation. I soon arrived at the end of the bridge, where I stood alone on the platform, looking at Devil's Throat in utter disbelief. While catching my breath, I was mesmerized by the spectacular sight of the massive falling waters in front of me. Instantly, I felt a cool mist surrounding the raging Falls. The sight was absolutely worthy of its esteemed designation as one of the World's Natural Wonders.

While the group arrived one by one, I specifically watched how this view overcame each tour member at first glance. There were lots of exclamations at the mighty forceful power of Iguazu Falls.

It made me very happy to see everyone enjoying this Wonder of the World.

While a local photographer took a group picture, the wind simultaneously blew away my hat and Matilda's. Both joined the crashing waters and lost them in the jungle. Being afraid something might happen to my precious needlepoint, I held on to it for dear life.

Note: most of the time, I carried the canvas with me, it only weighed less than a pound.
End of Note.

Even though no one could get enough of this stellar sight, we had to continue with our tour.

Reluctantly, the group started descending to the opposite side of the mountain towards the flats, there we were scheduled to take a boat ride with a close-up view of the Falls. This hike was different from the man-made walkway. Mother Nature's was naturally more daring.

During the downward walk, the view of the huge rock formations and smaller waterfalls that draped the hillside created a gorgeous sight. This radiant picturesque scene was indeed God's production. Continuing downhill, the pavement seemed to be somewhat safe but, at times, fairly steep.

Being careful was a must, so I also helped the group with the sections that dropped unexpectedly. The elders all made it, and I thanked the Creator for that.

While waiting our turn to enter the boat, we each received a plastic raincoat to protect us from getting wet. After the long wait, our boat was next in line. We carefully boarded. No one knew what was in store. The strength of the water was so powerful that the droplets could be felt from a distance. Meanwhile, the boat slowly and carefully approached the base of the massive waterfall. There was so much water all around us, the only thing to do was laugh a contagious laughter, which wouldn't stop. If that wasn't wet enough, it started to rain! More laughter.

Our raincoats proved to be ineffective. The force of the water practically destroyed them. We'd somehow survived nature's great energy and remained in good spirits. All of us continued to giggle hysterically at the soaking situation, as water poured from every direction. In a nutshell, no one's attire was dry, including our undergarments. Luckily, I protected my cloth bag by folding myself over and shielding it from constant splashes. Upon arrival at the end of the wet-and-wild ride, we were all drenched. I checked my needlepoint, and it was bone-dry. What a relief. Because we'd descended to have this exciting and adventurous boat-ride, the group needed to ascend towards our van (and then lunch).

At this time, Goldfinger, who believed that he was the richest person on this trip, and made sure everyone knew it. He couldn't take a single step upward. Francisco and Marco took each of his arms and propped them on their shoulders. They carried the incapacitated man all the way to the top. Without the help of the two men, he'd have to be detained at the bottom of the Falls. I sincerely hoped that this poor rich man tipped his two helpers and, if so, generously. Mr. Goldfinger should have been looking for a retirement home, instead of challenging Mother Nature.

I was happy and ready to climb towards the top. It wasn't easy because there were many irregular-sized stairs. I don't know what prompted me to count them, but I did.

By the time we all arrived back at the starting point, our clothes had dried out. Jacqueline waited for the group. I did not have the heart to tell her what she had missed, however, others did. To top it off, her husband didn't show any remorse for leaving his wife behind. This venturesome trip was not for her at all.

We grabbed a quick lunch and then headed back to the hotel for some free time. I used my precious moments on a local hike with other guests from the hotel.

During dinner Francisco instructed us regarding the next day.

He announced, "In the morning, bring all belongings to the van. We will be spending exciting hours at the

Brazilian side of the Falls, they are stunning. In the late afternoon, the van will take us to the airport for our short flight back to Buenos Aires."

We then congregated on the outside patio, reminiscing about the day's interesting sights and adventurous activities.

As an amusing exercise, I told the group, "I know how many steps we took up after the boat ride, I actually counted them, can anyone guess?"

One of the group members guessed it right on the money. To the best of my memory, there were 156 steps.

Before retiring for the night, I went to the front desk and requested that they send extra blankets to my new room. Hellen would probably blast the air conditioner tonight as well. I didn't want to confront her as she wouldn't oblige anyway (the selfish, classless being Hell-en from Hell).

A hot shower and then diving into layers of blankets was enough for me. After all, there had been plenty of activities during the day and the body needed a rest. Sleep appeared soon after. I actually had a nightmare, that I was sharing a room with Hell-en. Scary!

CHAPTER 18

Watch Out in Brazil

THURSDAY, FEBRUARY 12, IGUAZU FALLS—
ON OUR WAY TO THE Brazilian side.

Early in the morning, I went for a walk to relieve myself from the ice queen's negative energy all night long. I was glad that I switched rooms with Sally and hoped that she had a good night's sleep.

Very soon, I'd find out. On my way to the dining room, someone gave me a big hug from behind. Sally couldn't have been more thankful for my gesture of swapping rooms. Her appreciation made the sacrifice worth it.

After breakfast (some still making sandwiches), we proceeded to the van with all our carry-ons.

Back home, Alex was probably at the airport, waiting for his long flight to Buenos Aires.

I couldn't wait to greet him.

We arrived at the Brazilian border on time. My main concern for the group was safety.

After all, Francisco had told me more times than I wished to hear, "Watch out in Brazil! They will steal!"

That was engraved in my mind. I feared the worst and hoped for the best.

The line crossing from Argentina into Brazil was long but I suppose, worth the wait. When we finally arrived to the Falls entrance, all guest's vehicles had to be parked in the visitor's lot, the same as the day prior.

While still in the van, Francisco announced several times loud and clear, "Everyone, leave all your belongings in the van, the driver is the only one who has the key."

By now, it had been established that Francisco repeated himself over and again, this time was no different. While adjusting myself to exit the van, I placed the cloth bag with the needlepoint in it on my shoulders as I always did.

Again, Francisco said, "Leave all your belongings in the van the driver is the only one with the key."

At this point, I was a little confused. Do I take my cloth bag or not? I looked at Sam getting ready to exit the van, he placed a sophisticated camera lens on the floor underneath his seat. I thought, if he's leaving that expensive item behind, why not do the same with my cloth bag which looked like a shmata ("old garment" in Yiddish, but what's inside it was priceless to me). Okay, I decided to leave my needlepoint on the van, per Francisco's much-repeated instructions, so, I reluctantly inserted my personal item inside the net pocket designated to my seat. I always sat alone in the back row of the van.

All tour members, including Francisco and his friend, exited the van. I was the last one out the door. At that point and time, only the driver remained seated. We then entered the park's bus and headed towards the Falls. A few minutes later, and totally regretting leaving my needlepoint in the van, I desperately wanted to go back and fetch it, but the bus was already well on its way. I convinced myself that nothing would happen to my one-of-a-kind project.

Truly, the Brazilian side of the Falls were breathtaking. Many smaller clusters of falling waters were blended together, forming a collage-like scene. It was surely a sight to see and very different from its counterpart in Argentina.

At this time, Francisco asked me how I was enjoying the day.

I told him, "This place is out of this world, beautiful and unique! Unfortunately, I'm not enjoying it to the fullest because I left my needlepoint in the van. I should've taken it with me as I did yesterday and most of the time."

Francisco replied, "Conny, I'm sure it's safe and sound in the van, the driver is the only one that has access to get in."

How silly of me, Francisco was right for a change. I should be enjoying the spectacular scenery, with the nearly overwhelming 360-degree view.

All good things come to an end, and so Marco wrapped up his services with my group.

As we said our goodbyes, I handed him an envelope with his gratuities and said, "Thank you, I enjoyed every minute of your professional conduct and lots of knowledge, you are an incredible guide."

I wished I'd hired him for the whole trip, even though he didn't speak Hebrew, I would forfeit Francisco in a heartbeat if it meant we'd have Marco or someone alike.

At the end of the tour, the park's bus took us back to our van. Upon arrival, I rushed to be first.

It took a few minutes for the driver to arrive and open the door. As I entered the van, my anticipation was nerve-racking. I flew to my seat in the last row, only to discover that my cloth bag was not in the net pocket where I'd placed it just before exiting the van! Shivers went through my body. Shocked and shaken, I refused to believe the obvious.

I asked everyone, "Please look around your seats."

Perhaps my bag shifted or grew a pair of legs, so they could walk elsewhere in Brazil.

Everyone knew that the missing needlepoint was a big issue for me. I wasn't going to let this episode slide or entertain the idea that it might be gone forever. Hundreds of hours had gone into this labor of love. I looked all around the van, intent upon checking if there was something broken or evidence of forced entry from the windows or door. Everything was the same and intact inside the van.

I even looked under Sam's seat to check if his expensive camera lens had also vanished—it was in the same position since I saw it last. Extremely distraught, I went to the front of the van where Francisco was sitting next to the driver, he only spoke Portuguese.

Before opening my mouth, and knowing to filter each word, I told Francisco, "Please ask the driver if he had seen a cloth bag that was placed inside the net pocket of my seat in the last row."

In retrospect, I'm not sure whether Francisco asked him that sensitive question or something else. I don't know a word of Portuguese, so there was no way for me to confirm their conversation.

At that very moment, I had a strong feeling that some of the group members were getting uncomfortable and would accuse me of blaming the driver for the missing needlepoint. Not having concrete proof of wrongdoing (such as an eyewitness) meant I couldn't and never would make any accusations. Being wrong about that situation is not fair. A rule of mine: never accuse anyone of anything without evidence.

Having said that, and to offset a possible issue, I made sure that all the tour members heard me loud and clear as I said to Francisco for the second time, "Can you please **ask** the driver again if he knows the whereabouts of my cloth bag?"

Francisco seemingly asked the driver the question in Portuguese. The answer was disappointing news: nothing as such had been seen. Meanwhile, only two people in the bus knew the truth about my missing item. It was unspoken, of course.

Then Francisco suggested that I had probably left it somewhere in the Falls area or the souvenir shop that we'd visited. More bull nonsense from the unprofessional guide (who had the nerve to repeat his theory over and again).

I insisted that Francisco and I continue this ugly conversation somewhere other than inside the van.

I angrily said, "Let's go to the souvenir shop."

On the way I told him, "It could not be anywhere else other than the van. You gave us specific instructions multiple times to leave all belongings in the van, the driver is the only one with the key. I adhered to your directions and distinctly remember putting my needlepoint inside the net pocket of my seat. Furthermore, let me refresh your memory. Some hours ago, when you asked me how I was enjoying the Falls, my answer was negative because I left my needlepoint in the van."

He had no comment.

I continued, "While in the planning phase of the trip, you warned me what seemed to be a million times, 'tell your clients to be very careful in Brazil, people will steal.'

So, you should not have insisted that we leave our valuables behind in the van."

Again, he had no comments. We walked into the souvenir shop and asked if there were any lost items turned in. No luck (as if I didn't know). Before returning to the van, Francisco placed a call to the lost and found, in the main office, and inquired about my cloth bag. He was told, "Nothing as such was returned to us." (As if I didn't know.) Defeated, we both returned to the van.

To myself I thought, who else but the driver would be responsible for the disappearance of the needlepoint? My precious project was at the mercy of the only one with the key to the van.

Note: anyone who knows how to sew a button or mend a hem could complete the canvas in very little time, because it was near completion. When finished and framed a gorgeous piece of art would be on display. I was devastated and sad.

End of Note.

On that horrible account, we started the ride towards the airport for the short flight back to Buenos Aires.

My husband would probably be touching down at Aeropuerto Internacionales de Ezeiza just as we were landing at the domestic airport, but even that didn't make me feel better.

By the time we finally arrived at the hotel, all additional group members (who didn't join the Falls tour) had checked in and went to their rooms. Now from 14 tour members, we became 26.

My stepmom, Ruth (cute, petite, delicate, and a tough professional in her field of law), was part of the group. Marlin, her son, and my brother (sharing the same father), made sure that his mother would travel first-class. Francisco arranged a meet/assist ground attendant and a private transfer to the hotel. I was excited to see Ruth safe and sound. Delightfully, I welcomed her with a big hug.

While hugging my husband, his first question was, "What's up with the sour face?" I told him all about the missing needlepoint in full detail. He knew how hard I'd worked on it and understood my feelings.

We both agreed on the theory surrounding its disappearance, however, there was no proof. Oh well, hundreds of hours fell down, just like the falling waters of the Iguazu Falls.

I called every group member's room, advising them to meet me in the lobby at 7:00p.m. for orientation and then dinner. All arrived in a timely manner.

At the gathering, those who had recently arrived met Francisco for the first time, and all were pleasantly surprised to have a Hebrew-speaking guide. The newcomers blended nicely with the existing group.

How great that the surprise for Kiti and Pete was an astonishment, being reunited with their best friends Shlomo and Sharon was a great idea. The four were thrilled and elated to be together for this adventure, I couldn't be happier that the reunion had remained hush-hush.

Since the hotel only served breakfast, Francisco arranged a private room for dinner at a nearby restaurant. There we further became acquainted with one another.

On that note, the fourth day of the trip ended. I was heartbroken and humiliated. If that wasn't enough, the intense regret of not taking my needlepoint with me while touring the Falls on the Brazilian side was extremely disturbing and exhausting.

I started this trip in a very happy state of mind, but unfortunately, it did not last for long.

While lying down, before snoozing, my mind started to wander. I realized that Shlomo and his lovely wife, Sharon, never thanked me for the practically two-for-one Iguazu Falls tour. Also, days before Sam's birthday recognition was totally ignored. What an ungrateful set of tour members, not knowing when to say two little words, "Thank you." Even less, one word in Hebrew, "Toda."

A picture of my missing needlepoint.

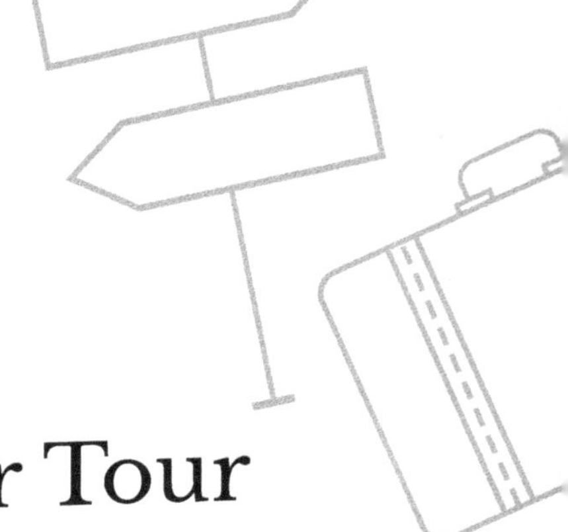

CHAPTER 19

The Dirty Water Tour

Friday, February 13, Buenos Aires, Argentina

I WAS HOPING FOR SOME good luck on the calendar's unluckiest day.

According to the first-tour contract between Francisco and me, the experience would include: A tour in the town of Tigre 8:30a.m. to 3:30p.m. The town is located by a river. We will navigate it for two hours. Lunch is not included.

Flashback to the planning phase of the trip: Some six months prior. Matilda told me, and I quote her, "My good friend just came back from Buenos Aires. She advised me to take the Gaucho Tour. It's a great experience, not to be missed." I relayed this important information to Francisco, he assured me that Tigre was all around much better than the Gaucho tour, including the price.

End of flashback.

The day began with breakfast and gossip (for those who thrived on it). Hellen and company made their lunches from the breakfast buffet, to which I thought, not again.

Soon after, we congregated in the lobby to take Francisco's first guided tour. I was nervous about how knowledgeable and professional he would be.

Two couples elected not to join the Tigre tour. They were Nate and Nancy from the UK along with, Marty and Miriam from Mexico. They apparently arranged to go elsewhere together for the day. The rest of us, including Francisco and his friend, boarded the tour bus. The drive was over an hour and extremely boring. The scenery, nothing to see. My feeling was not good, but I kept a pleasant face and forced a smile.

When the bus arrived at Tigre, we immediately boarded a rustic old boat that looked as if it transferred cargo in its heyday. What an introduction to Francisco's first guided tour. During the journey on the boat, we saw only ordinary homes on both sides of the riverbank. When arriving at the end, turning back and seeing the same monotonous scenery was a drag, and a totally pointless day.

Looking at everyone's body language, I saw great disappointment. This did not surprise me at all. Francisco's tour was not worth the effort, time, and money spent. The valuable hours on the river were gone with the wind. It wasn't long before Shlomo labeled this experience a "dirty water ride."

The highlight of this ailing tour was the welcoming fresh air and delightful breeze while on the aging and corroded boat. The two couples who elected not to join us were lucky on this Friday the 13th.

When the boat ride was finally over, we stopped at what seemed like a shabby eatery. Francisco knew the owners and arranged a lunch there (apparently so he could eat for free). Hellen and her peers went elsewhere to eat their sandwiches from the hotel's breakfast buffet. The rest of us sat in the restaurant's patio, because the weather was favorable near the water. The food was Italian inspired and quite good.

While preparing ourselves to leave, a strange noise from the opposite table alerted everyone. Oh, my goodness, Goldfinger regurgitated his entire lunch. This was the second health issue in two days, first, at the Falls, the knees could no longer take another step and now the stomach couldn't sustain the food he had for lunch. From the yucky sight, most of us dashed out to the awaiting bus.

After this failed tour, we started our boring drive back to the hotel.

The bus arrived around the same time as the two lucky couples who went elsewhere. While in the lobby and reminiscing about the useless tour, the lucky foursome informed us with great excitement that they had a wonderful time on the Gaucho tour, and a delicious lunch was included. My heart dropped. I approached Francisco and angrily confronted him regarding his lousy tour, which was a huge mistake, especially since I had told him about the Gaucho tour months before. Francisco heard the joyful comments from the two couples, and he couldn't even come up with a lie for his obvious screwup. So, disappearing from the group was the easiest option.

Needless to say, I felt bad for everyone on the dirty water ride. My apologies were extended several times, and I announced that I was going to greatly discount the worthless tour experience. That's the least I could do to make up for Francisco's lack of knowledge. After all, the responsibility for his performance fell on me. I hired him, and do believe in admitting fault, correcting mistakes, as well as compensating those who are affected.

Approaching Matilda was a must.

I told her, "I'm so sorry for not insisting and demanding that Francisco take us on the tour you recommended."

That evening and into the night, we had a full schedule, so I recommended some necessary rest.

The day seemed long and sadly short on pleasant hours. Most of the group went to their rooms for a siesta.

Francisco had arranged a Friday night service at the largest and oldest synagogue in Buenos Aires. Thereafter, a Friday night dinner at an upscale restaurant.

At 6:00p.m., the bus took us from the hotel to the synagogue in a timely manner. Patiently, we waited for the doors to open. The heat and humidity were most uncomfortable, but before long, a staff member came to greet us. First and foremost, the group was told, "Absolutely no photos of the synagogue's exterior and interior are to be taken." The building was artistic, stunning, and worthy of taking pictures, however, complying with all security measures was more important, and totally understandable.

Soon the doors opened. As we were about to enter the air-conditioned building, a security guard spotted Hellen taking photos. As a result, all of us were detained in the miserable heat. No one from Conny's group was allowed to step in the synagogue until all the pictures were deleted from the obnoxious woman's camera. The entire group grew frustrated. This useless female, with her silly laughter, had the chutzpah ("audacity" in Hebrew) to say, "My religious daughter needs to be informed that I am attending a Shabbat Eve service in Buenos Aires." Utter selfishness. By this time all of the group was sick and tired of her behavior. Class, she had, but below third.

Finally, we entered the air-conditioned synagogue and took our seats. The worship service was amazingly heartfelt. A choir sang an accompaniment to the prayers, the music sounded pleasant to the ears, all of us sat with smiles, soaking in each tune.

Most Friday night services, rabbis give an approximately 20-minute sermon. That night was no different. The presiding rabbi spoke multiple languages, including English, but he delivered his speech in Spanish only. Except for my husband and Francisco, no one else from our group understood what was being said, so we sat staring at the stunning artwork in the sanctuary. The rabbi knew that a group of 26 Jewish tourists would be attending his services. However, he had not been informed that practically all of our group didn't speak Spanish. Francisco knew of this situation and failed to make arrangements with the synagogue, so the rabbi could plan to speak some English as well. Another mistake from the useless and unprofessional tour guide.

Immediately after services, I went with Francisco's assistant/friend to pick up the challas (bread) and wine for dinner at the restaurant. The group and Francisco remained for Oneg Shabbat (gathering after the services).

Note: Kiti later told me, "While you were away, the group collected money for the synagogue. However, somehow, Francisco was in possession of the envelope. I hope that he forwarded it to a staff member, I don't really trust him and regretted not giving the collection to a synagogue administrator myself."

I told Kiti, "That was a nice thing to do."

End of note.

Meanwhile, Francisco's assistant and I drove to the restaurant. The private room on the second floor was arranged beautifully with a huge U-shaped table, and the lovely decor provided a classy atmosphere. I quickly started to prepare the amenities that I'd brought from home especially for the Shabbat Eve feasts (during the trip, there would be three of them). Within a half an hour, the group walked to the banquet room, all were pleasantly surprised to see what was prepared for them. The Shabbat candles were lit by one of the ladies, Alex did the Kiddush (prayers), and we all sang Sabbath songs. It was a very yiddishkeit (Jewish atmosphere) evening in the heart of Buenos Aires.

The restaurant's service was incredible, the food had enough variety to meet everyone's palate, and the chef was to be commended. The menu had a set price; thus, everyone would pay the same, and the appropriate tip would apply. But why should things go smoothly? After the bill was given to Francisco, I collected money from everyone. Francisco assumed that the amount was correct, but it was $60 short. He checked and rechecked, still no go—$60 missing.

The head waiter noticed the problem. He approached me, gestured to Jack, and said, "That person ate all of his dinner, thereafter complained about the food, and asked for another meal with more bread, again he cleared his second plate."

I went to Jack and confronted him about the restaurant's allegation.

The jerk loudly said, "I absolutely refuse to pay the full amount, the first plate was no good."

So, I asked him, "Why did you finish the food?"

He had no answer and did not shell out the missing $60 to cover his second meal.

I was so tempted to tell this creature off, but we had enough negativity for one day. I elected to restrain my urge and not escalate the tension. There was no sense to continue checking where the money went, it's obvious that the hedonistic ingrate was responsible for the missing amount.

At this time, all of us were exhausted and agitated regarding this ugly scene.

Finally, Alex reached for his pocket, and pulled out $60 to cover the amount owed by a pig called Jack, then my generous husband declared, "Let's go."

In a righteous world, Jack should have paid for three dinners, but no, he gorged on two, and his wife ate one, making a total of three, and only paid for two plates while refusing to tip as well. Some cheater.

What should have been remembered as a sweet Shabbat Eve dinner gathering, went down as a bitter end on this unlucky Friday the 13th, thanks to the thorn from Arizona and Hell-en (from Hell), who made us go through the scorching sun earlier in the day.

Rather late, we arrived at the hotel, somewhat disappointed. I was worn out while being disgusted with some tour members, as if Francisco's wasn't bad enough.

Before retiring for the night, I wished, hoped, and prayed for better days with the unprofessional guide as well as a number of unruly group members. We were only in the early stages of the trip, but I had a strong feeling that my problems had only just begun.

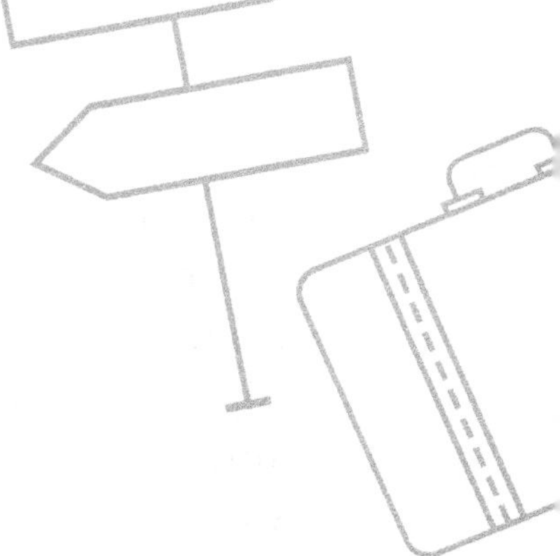

CHAPTER 20

Tango, Anyone?

Saturday, February 14 (Valentine's Day), Buenos Aires, Argentina

THE TOUR CONTRACT BETWEEN FRANCISCO and myself stated: Visiting the highlights of the city, 9:00a.m. to 4:00p.m. Places to visit include: Pink House, government buildings, Recoleta Cemetery, Puerto Madero, Caminito, La Boca, and Palermo. Lunch is not included.

According to Francisco's plan, it was set to be an interesting day in the city known for fine food, drinks, culture, and of course, tango. During breakfast, Francisco signaled me to meet him outside.

I'd already guessed the issue, so before he started to talk, I said, "I know what you are going to complain about, the making of sandwiches from the breakfast buffet. Don't worry, I will take care of the situation. You have my word."

We then returned to the breakfast room.

I later consulted with Alex, and together, we agreed to leave a fair amount of money at the front desk upon check-out the next day. We hoped this would cover the extra food that some uncultured tour members made lunch from the breakfast buffet. It was important to make it right, especially since this is a mom-and-pop operation. Our reservation was for bed and breakfast, not including lunch.

I did not expect many group members to join today's tour simply because the previous day had been nonsense over dirty water, but I was pleasantly surprised, more than half were waiting to enter the bus. The driver drove along the main boulevard towards the city center. We viewed the Pink House, which serves as a mansion and office for Argentina's president, then a continuation to the famous Recoleta Cemetery, there we exited the bus.

The walk was quite interesting, unusual, and a bit spooky. No wonder this site was so famous, María Eva Duarte de Perón is buried there. She was the first lady of Argentina from 1946 until her death in 1952, also famous for her championing women's suffrage and working-class rights in Argentina.

Next, we headed to a restaurant for lunch. Francisco bragged how great the eatery would be.

I hoped for a simple, clean, and quick place, so we'd have more time for touring. But no, the incompetent guide chose a lavish restaurant, and he was excited to tell us that they serve a free piece of cake to anyone having a birthday that week. Francisco knew that Sam had a birthday a few days prior. In order to qualify for the sweet treat, identification was required for proof. How infantile, we are adults on a once-in-a-lifetime trip, not kids attending a birthday party at Chuck E. Cheese.

After an hour, those who ate their sandwiches at a nearby park came to see if we'd finished our meals at the restaurant. No such luck, while I was on edge during the entire lunch. We only had two days in Buenos Aires. The first day has gone with the lovely wind, wasted on a lousy tour, and now, for a lousy free piece of cake, we were exhausting time on the second day, as well. Waiting for the free piece of cake took more time than lunch, on a day that already had a very tight schedule.

After nearly an hour and a half, I demanded that Francisco wrap up and get the group back on the bus. There was still much to see and do, however, now the seven-hour tour probably would decline to less than five hours. I was furious.

Finally, everyone was out the door. Having no choice, we rushed a lot, saw a little of Buenos Aires's highlights, and even missed some of the sites on the tour contract. As a result, additional mistakes to deal with, and plenty of complaints came my way from some of the group members, rightfully so. Another tour to be discounted.

Because it was Valentine's Day, which fell on a Saturday, Francisco arranged for an optional night event: dinner and a tango show. Those who wanted to participate paid him directly. I thought, what a great idea for the group and more revenue for the lousy guide. All the members joined the evening event. After all, this is Argentina, where tango rules, especially on a day for lovers. The dinner was standard, but the show was above expectations due to the superb talent and fantastic legs of the dancers.

Returning to the hotel after a busy day and night, everyone seemed to be exhausted, and I was wiped out from trying to keep up with all the incidents that went wrong. The feedback from the group regarding the two days of touring, was poor. Of course, I agreed. Francisco's mistakes were getting on the expensive side and on my nerves.

CHAPTER 21

Land Meets an Ocean

Sunday, February 15

Tying up Buenos Aires, Argentina, heading out onto the Atlantic Ocean.

It was the last breakfast at the hotel, and it would be the first lunch on board the ship (no more making sandwiches from the hotel's breakfast buffet, thank goodness). After bringing our luggage to the hotel's storage room, we had a free morning. Francisco suggested that we take a short walk to a flea market not far from the hotel.

He assured us that it would be interesting, entertaining, and coincidentally, only open on Sundays. So, all of us went. The artwork, touristy trinkets, and old artifacts appeared on display. Most of all, we enjoyed the tango dancers performing between the cafes and vendors.

Around noon, our encounter with the locals wrapped up, as did our stay in Buenos Aires. Upon arrival back at the hotel, Francisco and the driver were already loading our luggage onto the bus for a transfer to the pier.

While we were on our way to the ship, Francisco hopped in a taxi, heading for the airport to catch a short flight, visiting his parents, they lived in Punta del Este (the ship's first port of call).

The following morning, he'd guide us on a city and vicinity day tour.

The ride to the pier was a perfect time to inform the group about dining arrangements and some other matters.

I announced, "Your room steward will provide a list of activities on a daily basis, as well as eatery options for breakfast, lunch, and snacks. The choices will be plentiful. Choose what best suits you. For dinner, a notice will be placed in your cabin, advising you of your dining room, name and table number. You also have two additional options, the ship's standard buffet, which transitions to dinner around 6:00p.m., and one of the three specialty restaurants but for an additional charge."

Note: while planning the trip, I asked everyone to indicate which timeframe best meets your preference for early dinner at 6:15p.m. or late dinner at 8:15p.m. Accordingly, all of you answered me. Half of the group fancied earlier, and the other desired later dining. The main show would be featured twice in conjunction with the two dinner sittings. All understood.

End of note.

It was a crammed day between packing, visiting the flea market, transferring to the pier, then standing in a long line checking in and again unpack. After many months of preparation, the 13-day South America/Rio Carnival Parade cruise had finally arrived.

With hefty appetites, a stop at the buffet made sense.

After lunch, and before dispersing to do whatever each wished (rest, unpack, roam around the ship), I took the group to show them where our meeting spot would be when exiting the ship or any other scheduled gatherings.

I made sure to emphasize the importance of remembering this specific location. It would make life simple and easy for the next 13 days. Then everyone went their own way, and I had an important agenda to address.

I called security to ask if the head officer was Israeli. I was told yes. That was music to my ears.

I further asked, "May I speak to him?"

The operator put me on hold. Within a few minutes, a very distinctive voice came on the line and said, "This is David. May I help you?"

In Hebrew, I introduced myself and informed him about my group being mostly Hebrew speaking. I then asked, "David, may I please see you for a few moments?"

His reply was, "Sure, but I only have five minutes to spare."

I answered, "That's all I need."

He told me where to wait for him.

While waiting in the main lobby, I spotted a handsome, tall, refined young man with an impressive uniform and name tag. A handshake was appropriate.

I worked up the chutzpah and said, "For my group, can you meet us after the late show tonight?"

He happily answered, "Yes, I can. I'll be looking for all of you at the card room on the tenth floor, 10:00p.m., sharp."

I replied, "Can't wait and thank you so much."

Before we parted, David gave me his private phone number and stated, "Call me anytime, or just say shalom."

I was the happiest camper on the high seas. I then went to my cabin and called everyone with the following message, "Please avail yourself at 10:00p.m. tonight for a very special gathering in the card room on the tenth floor. Do not miss this meeting." I had the strongest feeling that the group would be pleasantly surprised.

Approximately 6:00p.m., the ship set sail for an overnight voyage to Punta del Este, Uruguay.

At 6:30p.m., I went to the dining room to check on the 13 early diners. There were no complaints, in fact, they were all happy. Thus, I was happier. I reminded them to meet me at the card room after their show.

Some asked, "Why?"

I replied, "A pleasant surprise will await."

At 8:15p.m. (after the early show), Ruth, Alex, and I went to the dining room, joining the late diners.

Everyone was pleased. Following dinner, I said, "Let's go to the card room."

By 10:00p.m., all of the tour members (Hebrew speaking) gathered there. David greeted us with a big smile and a bigger shalom. The group was pleasantly surprised and overwhelmed to be around an Israeli officer. An immediate sense of chemistry filled the room. We then sat in the circle seating arrangement that David had put together. He explained in Hebrew all about his duties onboard the ship. With no exception we gave him our undivided attention. The questions were plentiful with responsive and accommodating answers. The evening's atmosphere was second to none, and we couldn't get enough from the charming head of security. David made us feel as if he was our personal security officer. The level of pride was sky-high, having such a fine Israeli citizen in command of the ship's safety. I cannot begin to express how meaningful and heartfelt the time turned out.

At the end of the evening, which was way after midnight, I thanked David for the valuable hours he'd spent with my group.

He told me again, "Be in touch at any time. You already have my direct contact. I will avail myself to you and your group around my busy schedule."

Amazing! What a positive change from the negative issues with Francisco.

Before retiring for the night, I reminded the group to meet me by 9:00a.m. at our meeting place for the tour in Punta del Este. I didn't expect full attendance for Francisco's third tour. So, day one of the cruise ended on a positive note, knowing that David was responsible for the safety measures on the high seas.

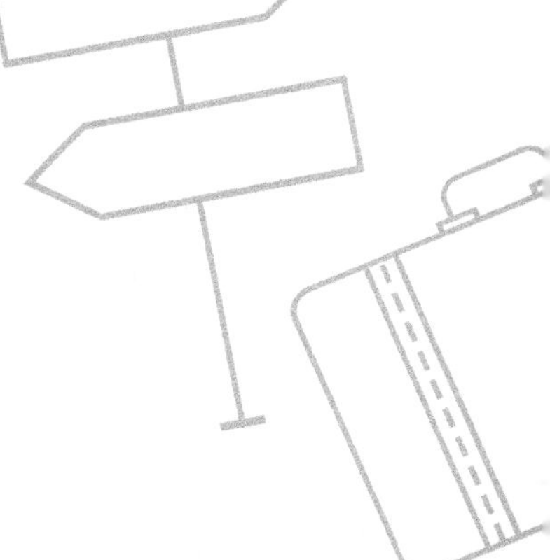

CHAPTER 22

A Charming City

Monday, February 16, Punta del Este, Uruguay

THE SHIP WILL BE DOCKED from 7:00a.m. to 6:00p.m.

Note: Regarding the above information, when a ship arrives at her ports of call, the cruise company posts at the exit (of the ship) the following:

1. Name of the city/country
2. Time of departure, 'set sail'

It is extremely important to be on time, as the cruise line is not obliged to wait for late arrivals. Being tardy means chasing the ship to her next destination, at your own expense.
End of note.

The tour contract between Francisco and me is as follows:

- We will visit both towns, Punta del Este and Piriápolis
- Casapueblo Museum
- Punta Ballena, La Barra Bridge

- Hands with fingers, meeting Point of the River and the Ocean
- Lunch is included at the rain forest in Piriapolis.

Truly, I worried about the fate of tour number three, but I was counting on an old saying, "Third time is the charm."

How did the group feel about another tour with Francisco? Not very well. His first one was a complete failure, and the second? Not up to par. I had no idea how many members would trust Francisco enough to join the tour today. I truly wondered.

At breakfast, I informed the group that Uruguay's department of agriculture had strict laws banning outside food from entering their territory for biological reasons. In addition, security may randomly check for any sign of the rules being broken. Hellen and company were not happy. Too bad.

At 9:00a.m., I was surprised again, that almost everyone gathered at our designated area to disembark the ship for the day and reunite with Francisco. I supposed that the discounts I would provide, due to the guide's lousy guidance, was reason enough to risk the possibility of another failed tour.

Stepping out of the ship, the group was greeted with perfect weather. Proceeding to the outside perimeter of the port took no more than five minutes. Francisco was there, awaiting our arrival. For a change, he was not accompanied by plus-one (so I thought).

We boarded the bus and made our way to the seats. Before the driver started the ignition, Francisco announced loud and clear, "Welcome to beautiful Punta del Este, my favorite city in Uruguay." He proudly told us that he has two surprises: The first, "My mother, father, uncle, and auntie are on the bus. They're sitting all the way in the back." We all turned our heads to politely acknowledge them (some more freebies on my account—today, it was his family).

Then he enthusiastically announced, the second surprise, "The van driver from the Iguazu Falls tour called me with good news! He found Conny's needlepoint on a bench in the Iguazu Falls (Brazil's side). It's being held at the office with the manager, Bernardo."

I did not ask a single question because I knew very well that it had not been found on any bench in the entire country of Brazil. My cloth bag with the needlepoint in it was left in the van, per Francisco's multiple instructions. His story was obviously untrue, so here was lie number one for the day. However, challenging him would be a waste of time and energy.

Outwardly, I jumped for joy, and adamantly stated, "I want to compensate the driver. Please give me his address."

Francisco replied, "I personally gave him something already."

This marked the second lie of the day. Geographically, it's impossible to do as he said, considering that the Brazilian side of the Falls are some seventeen hundred miles from Buenos Aires, where the entire group (including Francisco) had been for three days straight. Between that and his flight to Punta del Este (on the fourth day), he could not have possibly and personally given the driver anything anywhere.

I let Francisco's false story go, as I had no desire being subjected to any more lies on behalf of my personal item. I still needed to recover my needlepoint, and challenging him would not be the answer. Trusting this character was a thing of the past. I felt relieved, but I wasn't going to celebrate until I saw the canvas with my own eyes. I was thankful and showed polite appreciation.

We toured charming Punta del Este and Piriápolis all morning. The two cities were perfect for family vacations. Francisco knew their histories and vital information, so he performed well as a guide in his familiar territory.

Our next stop before lunch was at a farm. It had a small zoo with local animals. A nervous monkey was jumping all around his cage, he did all kinds of funny tricks in hopes that we would toss him some food. This monkey had us laughing hysterically. From all the laughter, our appetite for lunch increased, so we went to the farm's restaurant.

Hellen had to do something sickening as always. This time, it was really disgusting. While a platter of hors d'oeuvres was being served, Hellen picked up one, took a bite, apparently not liking its taste, she pulled the food out of her mouth and placed the remaining appetizer right back onto the tray. Her teeth marks were apparent on the rejected half. For goodness's sake, how low can she go? A few of us witnessed this repulsive act and just shook our heads in disbelief. The monkey had more manners than her.

After lunch, two singers (who were a married couple) performed for the group. Both were extremely humble and had incredible talent. Their voices were awesome, worthy of professional opera singers. We thoroughly enjoyed them.

Then Francisco dressed up as a silly, dizzy, confused clown. I had a chuckle thinking that he didn't have to try very hard for the role. The music was lively, and most of the group danced to Latin sounds, perfectly fitting the momentum of a pleasant afternoon.

While the dancing went on, I did not participate. Paperwork awaited me. I heard Hellen asking Alex to dance with her. He flatly refused, which was rude and unlike him. My husband would never insult a soul, so this rejection was a surprise to me. Later, I asked him why the refusal in such a harsh manner?

He replied, "I'm just sick and tired of her despicable behavior."

I couldn't argue with that.

Meanwhile, Francisco earned points thanks to his excellent performance as a guide and for the phenomenal entertainment that went on for some two and half hours. The day was fun, funny, festive, and fully fabulous.

Reluctantly, all of us began preparing ourselves to head for the ship. Soon, we boarded the bus, and on our way we went. During the drive, I approached Francisco to discuss the return of my needlepoint.

He told me, "Conny, your needlepoint is safe and sound. It's in the hands of Bernardo, the manager at the Falls' lost and found on the Brazilian side. Using Brazil's mail system is not safe because it could go missing again, so the next time I have a client visiting that region, I will ask that person to bring your needlepoint back to the States."

I said, "Thank you. I'll provide a FedEx number for the delivery to my home."

We arrived at the ship an hour prior to set sail. There was ample time to rest before the evening's activities. The group exchanged shaloms and adioses with Francisco. Our next meeting with him would be in six days at the port of Rio de Janeiro, his favorite city in Brazil. He didn't forget to tell us once again that he had been to the Rio Carnival Parade 16 times in the last 16 years.

At dinner, just as my hot plate was served, a complaint was brought to my attention, by one of the nicest couple, Solomon and Sue. Apparently, they were greatly disturbed by the excessive noise from the air conditioner outside their cabin.

They further told me, "It was impossible to sleep last night due to the noise. The maintenance department failed to rectify the problem and our attempt to switch cabins was unsuccessful."

This problem didn't sit well with me. I immediately excused myself from the table and dashed down to the guest relations desk. I spoke with the supervisor regarding my client's complaint. The problem was finally corrected.

Returning to the dining room some 20 minutes later, I told Solomon and Sue, "At your convenience, go to guest relations. The key to your new cabin is awaiting. In the event you'll need help moving your belongings, a housekeeping attendant will assist you."

They couldn't have been happier and more appreciative. By then, my dinner was on the cool side, but my heart felt warm knowing that I had successfully resolved their problem, so they could enjoy their cabin and the rest of the trip.

From the beginning, we had noticed that Hellen generally ordered multiple entrées. She wouldn't necessarily eat it all and apparently couldn't care less about wasting food. After the dessert menus were given, we each ordered one of our favorite sweets. To the waiter's amazement, Hellen ordered all five dessert choices.

I will never forget the look on the waiter's face as he asked her, "Are you on a special diet?"

She gave him a sarcastic look.

Someone from the group asked, "Why five desserts?"

She answered, "With my money, I can order and eat as much as I want."

We all looked at each other, silently cracking up at this pathetic behavior.

When her five desserts arrived, the table was saturated with sweet plates.

I quietly told Alex and Ruth, "Let's move on and have our desserts at the buffet."

Both happily agreed, and we had a little sweetness added to our palates.

After the main show, I arranged a get-together in the '60s-themed lounge—my favorite era. We danced to its romantic music and told nostalgic stories from our teen years. David joined us for some more interesting and enjoyable conversation. Indeed, the evening turned out to be a success.

This wrapped up the day's outstanding activities and happenings. I hoped that the rest of this trip would be easy and pleasant like today. Wishful thinking, I'm allowed to hope.

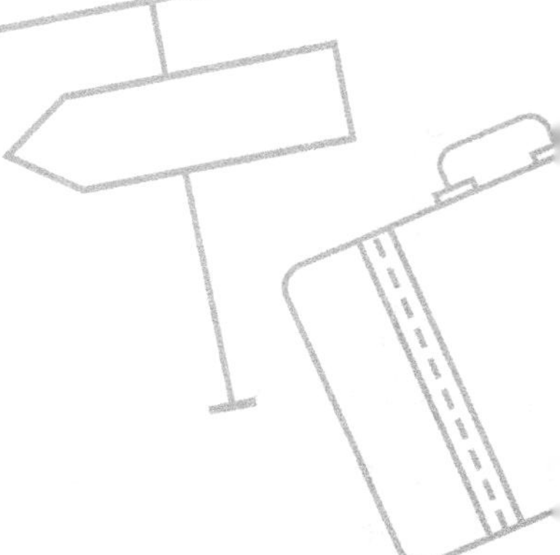

CHAPTER 23

People Will Talk

Tuesday, February 17, A Day at Sea

Apparently, word had gotten around the ship regarding Francisco's tour to Punta del Este. His tour excelled and delivered more than expected. It was indeed a hit. I compared the itinerary with the ship's tour desk, and theirs was the standard highlights of the city. I thought, Finally, he's getting it together, and hopefully, there will be no more problems and mistakes on the next three tours.

Because of this success, random passengers approached me asking if they could join my next tour, which would be Santos and São Paulo, Brazil, in two days. From the ones who were interested, I took their cabin numbers and said, "I'm not sure if our existing bus can be changed to a bigger one, however, I will contact my source, and when I have an answer, you'll hear from me at once."

I called Francisco to tell him about the situation.

He answered, "I'll check with my friend Jose about the change and email you back."

In the evening, I received an email from Francisco. The answer was, "None of the larger buses are available." I found this answer to be very strange, but I had no control and couldn't do anything about what seemed to be a lie, this time from Francisco's colleague.

As promised, I contacted the ones who were still interested and advised them: "I could not upgrade to a bigger bus, however, come with me when I'll be meeting the tour guide, perhaps something can be done. No promises, the price is pending," I further told them when and where to meet the group.

I took advantage of the much-deserved full free day. It had been over a week of daily activities since the start of the trip. I'd earned some 'me time' while the ship sailed towards the horizon. There was lots to do, casino, bingo, shopping, dancing, cooking lessons, trivia, karaoke, or one could choose to do nothing at all.

Travel agents, bringing a group onboard a ship and passengers who are elite members (meaning frequent sailors), will normally be recognized and appreciated by the cruise line. There are several ways to show appreciation, for instance providing certain perks, such as invitations to special events and private parties, shops, salon, spa, and other amenities throughout.

Having said that, the next time I went down to my cabin, I received an invitation to a private cocktail party that would take place the following evening at 5:00p.m. This event allowed the elite cruisers to personally meet the captain and his officers. I was sure that this gathering would be interesting, informative, and enjoyable, so I requested permission to bring the group along with me. My request was granted. Immediately, I invited everyone. The response was overwhelming. Conny's group would gladly attend. I hoped that the unruly tour members would change their mind by tomorrow and not attend.

During the late afternoon, I went to my cabin to rest and prepare for the evening's activities. No sooner after I arrived, the phone rang. It was Kiti, asking if I would do her hair.

I said, "Sure, come on up."

Throughout the cruise, she was the only one taking my offer.

Dinner was delicious, and the show, better than expected.

By 10:00p.m., we gathered in the Blue Lounge.

I informed the group, "Tonight, there is an anniversary celebration for Marty and Miriam. We did the usual card signing and gift giving."

Before long, the band realized that we're a Hebrew-speaking crowd, so they played the hora (a traditional Jewish dance) on and on. David followed the well-recognized music, and with the noise, it was hard to miss Conny's group. He joined us, so the good times continued on and on.

After the band concluded their performance, David volunteered to share a bit about his personal life. He was living in the metropolitan area of Tel Aviv, barely 30 years old, and a bachelor. At his tender age, being responsible for maintaining all safety protocols on the full ship, thousands of passengers, and the crew, was incredible. I am sure that some of the women having daughters around his age wished to have one like David as their son-in-law, including me.

(Fast forward years later my wish came true.)

The time was close to midnight, and we were still enjoying Dave's company. No one wanted to retire just yet.

At the end of the night Marty and Miriam didn't forget to graciously thank me for their simhah (celebration in Hebrew), unlike Sam, Shlomo, and Sharon.

Later on, and with drooping eyes, we decided to turn in. It had been a day, evening, and night well spent.

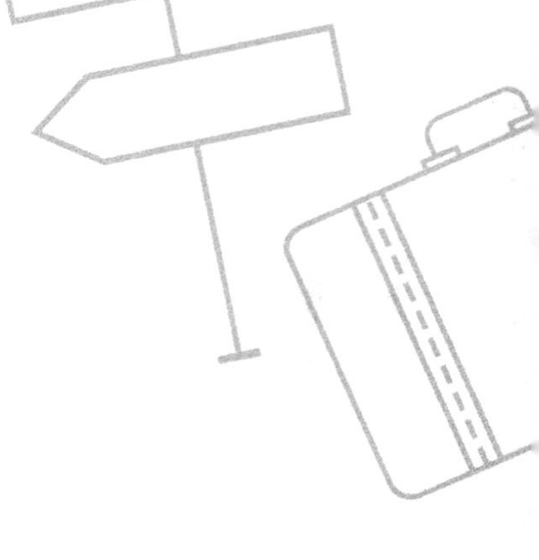

CHAPTER 24

A Lovely Day in a Pretty Port

Wednesday, February 18, Porta Bello, Brazil

THE SHIP WILL BE DOCKED from 8:00a.m. to 5:00p.m. The sun was shining brightly, and conditions were just right for outdoor activities. Some group members elected to walk around the vicinity for local shopping and browsing, others wanted to venture the pretty island, while the rest lounged by the ship's pool.

We were 12 that agreed to hire an open jeep with a driver. The first attraction was a waterfall. A brisk walk was required to arrive at its natural cascading waters. There was a sign posted, "1.5 meters (5 feet) deep, (my world) swim at your own risk." The water was crystal clear. I suddenly got the urge to jump in the inviting pool. After all, it was a hot day, and I fancied doing something wet and wild.

Three seconds later, I found myself totally submerged in the pool. If ever I'd been truly revived, that was the time and place. Pete jumped in right after me. We laughed at our silly and impulsive actions. I'm sure that the old vibers thought I was nuts, but adventure, discovery, and exploration is up my alley, not theirs. Alex and Ruth were not surprised, they knew me and my capabilities.

After this experience, we all walked along a beautiful forest path for 30 minutes or so. By then, my clothes had a chance to dry. Our break for lunch was about an hour long. For this designated time, each one did as they desired. Some got their feet wet while walking along the water's edge, others walked around the little village and ate an early lunch. The three of us just had some ice cream, and I chose to go for a jog on the wet sand. I love the touch of the breaking waves. Alex and Ruth rented two beach chairs for relaxation.

We returned to the ship and had a light late lunch then a nap to restore our energy for the evening, which would be full of activities, starting with an eloquent cocktail party.

I hoped that the ones who'd exhibited low-class behavior would do something other than attend a classy gathering.

By 5:00p.m., every single person had arrived at the private party (darn it). The event started with the captain introducing his officers one by one. They spoke about their duties and the new fleet coming in the near future. After David's speech, my group clapped and cheered him Israeli style (somewhat loud) because we were so proud and fond of him. Time for questions and answers was allotted. I was impressed with the interesting questions posed by some of my group members. The officer's replies were delivered with enthusiasm and expertise.

The cocktails and hor d'oeuvres were delicious and plentiful. My attention focused on Hellen, who devoured the various delicacies. Thank goodness she enjoyed them and did not return half-eaten portions to the serving plate, as she did in Punta del Este.

Throughout this journey, I'd noticed that liquor and wine were rarely ordered by any of the tour members, but at this event, the consumption of alcohol was somewhat popular, especially with a handful of people.

Soon after the cocktail party was over, Miriam approached me and said, "Tonight, Marty and I are not joining you for dinner. We're going to have our meal alone elsewhere."

I asked her why, she answered, "Hellen's loud nonsense and wild behavior gives us a headache. We want a relaxing evening."

I couldn't argue with that. Hell-en could give a headache to anyone at any given time.

After dinner, there was a talent show starring the passengers. Some people showed real acting ability, passion, and talents. There was a dance competition, and the winner took home a bottle of champagne.

As the long and busy evening came to a closure, I suggested that everyone get a full night's rest because the next day, we'd have an intensive schedule in Santos and São Paulo.

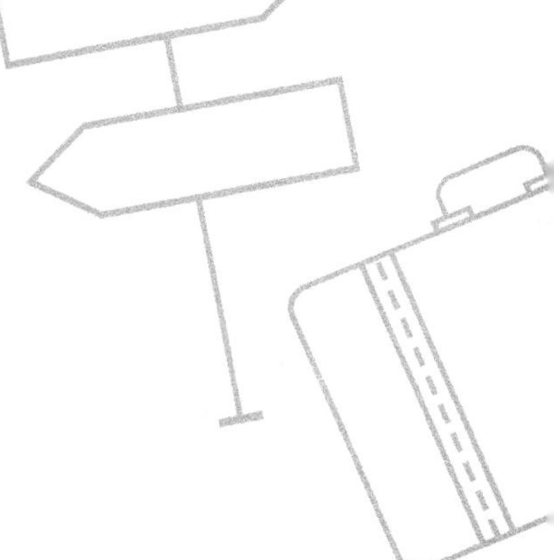

CHAPTER 25

So Far, the Worst

Thursday, February 19, São Paulo/Santos, Brazil

THE SHIP WILL BE DOCKED from 8:00a.m. to 6:00p.m. The above two cities are listed as such on all the printed materials associated with tours and ports of call. It would be reasonable enough to believe that São Paulo and Santos border each other, but they do not. In fact, more than 52 miles separate the two cities, furthermore, the ship docked in Santos because São Paulo does not have a seaport. This incorrect posting would result in a huge problem.

The tour contract between Francisco and I stated: A full day tour of Santos and São Paulo 8:30a.m. to 5:30p.m. You will see the highlights of both places with your bilingual guide. Lunch is not included.

A quick reminder: Francisco had told me from the beginning of our planning that he knew nothing about Santos or São Paulo, so he hired his colleague/friend Jose, a local travel agent and tour organizer, to plan today's tour. This meant that the colleague was Francisco's subagent, thus, all responsibility and liability from Jose's arrangements would fall on Francisco. In the same regard, I was responsible and liable for my subagent, Francisco.
End of reminder.

All 26 of us (plus the tagalongs, seven couples) congregated in our designated spot to disembark the ship. We then stood in a long line for passport control. Visa and non-visa citizens were crammed into one line, instead of the norm, two lines. At that time, US citizens required a visa to enter Brazil, Israeli citizens did not. As a result of this obstacle, we were delayed for nearly an hour to enter Brazil.

Our day was so busy and tightly scheduled with sightseeing in two major cities, I wondered if Jose took into consideration that time would be of the essence. While waiting to cross passport control and all logistics, I started to worry that the morning was quickly ticking away.

Finally, my group completed the border procedure, which was much more complicated than entering the Brazilian side of the Iguazu Falls.

We then proceeded to the independent pickup area. A lovely young lady stood nearby with a sign reading, "Conny's Group." She was presentable and looked professional as a guide.

Our introduction was a hefty handshake, and she said, "My name is Maritza."

We bonded right away.

First and foremost, I asked her about the 14 tagalongs who wanted to join us. Maritza claimed that there were plenty of buses bigger than the one we had, and they were available, but she couldn't change the bus with 30 seats that was already assigned and waiting for us.

This conflicted with my conversation just two days earlier when Francisco had told me, "Absolutely no larger buses will be available."

Somebody had lied, either Francisco or Jose. I ventured to say that it was Jose this time.

Maritza suggested hiring a driver with a van.

She explained, "They'll follow our bus, and it shouldn't take more than ten minutes to make arrangements."

The tagalongs agreed, and I paid the extra charge.

While waiting for the van to be delivered, I noticed that the tour bus had a dingy-looking exterior.

I then stepped inside to check it out. Wow, I couldn't believe my eyes. The interior seemed shabby and outdated, the seats displayed wear and tear, the floor was dusty and cracked, the window coverings were dilapidated. The restroom—I didn't want to enter. Overall, it looked like an old local bus and not one for tourists.

As promised by Maritza, the van was ready in a timely manner. After everyone situated themselves on the full bus, there was no space for me, so I went to the van and sat with the tagalongs. We started towards our sightseeing in Santos.

From my seat, I noticed that every time the bus stopped for a red light, its engine would shut off and the driver barely managed to restart it. My feelings about the tour were simply rotten.

The only interesting attraction in Santos was the field where the world-famous soccer player, Edson Arantes do Nascimento (known as Pelé, the pride of Brazil) practiced there. This highlight was worth exiting the bus and van to take photos, especially for the ones who are obsessed with soccer.

On the way back to our vehicles, some of the tour members who were riding on the bus complained to me that the air conditioner was not working properly, and the microphone seemed to be an upscale version of a toy. Maritza had to raise her voice each time she spoke. Not surprisingly, the lousy old bus came with lousy features because it was obvious by now that the tour had been planned by a lousy planner (Jose, just like Francisco).

We were on our way to São Paulo. I was fearful of what awaited us next.

While following the bus on the highway and knowing its poor condition, my gut feeling about this tour grew worse by the minute and my intuition pointed to a very bad day, but I kept all the negative feelings to myself and proceeded with a fake smile. The scenery of a beautiful forest that stretched between the two cities made the ride somewhat delightful.

Noon was slowly approaching, and we were nowhere near São Paulo. How could the group visit the huge city with a break for lunch when nearly half of the day was already gone to the dickens?

Bearing in mind that this was the year that São Paulo was rated the biggest city in the world. Time was short, and I wondered how long it would be before we'd arrive at our destination. Though we were getting closer, there was a significant traffic jam on the way, so more time wasted.

Being aware that the air conditioner is broken I was so concerned about the heat circulating in the old bus, and how many people were sweating. What a horrible situation.

Finally, the long drive was nearly over. We saw a sign that said, "Welcome to São Paulo!" The bus driver found a circular area where both vehicles could park.

While exiting the van, I heard loud chaos and commotion coming from those who'd already disembarked the bus. Voices over louder voices shouted at Maritza.

I wiggled my way through the madness and asked her, "What in the world is going on?!"

Maritza said, "During the bus ride, I briefed the group that we are only going to the Jewish Federation for a lecture, and lunch to be purchased, there's no time for anything else. All hell broke loose, because none of the tour members wanted to attend a lecture at any federation, Jewish or not. They wanted to visit and experience São Paulo, the biggest city in the world. Furthermore, the added heat on the bus fueled their frustration." I was livid.

This information was certainly news to me. The group knew that we would be touring the highlights of Santos and the energetic city, São Paulo. Everyone was justified, no question about it.

At this point, Maritza and I took out our contracts and itineraries. Mine from Francisco read as follows:
"A full day tour of Santos and São Paulo, 8:30a.m. to 5:30p.m. You will see the highlights of both places with your bilingual guide and lunch is not included in the price."

Maritza's contract received from Francisco's colleague Jose read as follows:
"Drive through Santos to São Paulo. Attend a lecture at the Jewish Federation. Lunch to be purchased. Drive back to the ship."

We were both totally shocked. This was not what I had agreed to, paid for, and signed. Francisco and Jose had two completely different contracts and itineraries.

Maritza loudly exclaimed, "Oh my goodness. In all my years of guiding, I've never seen anyone attempt such a bizarre and impossible tour, such as Francisco's itinerary."

I told her, "Please put what you just stated in writing."

She answered, "I absolutely will do so, just as soon as things settle down."

This was beyond a mistake. Francisco and his colleague, two nitwits had not synchronized their planning, or something more nefarious was up. Perhaps Jose wanted to make a quick buck by providing a cheap and ailing bus that had limited number of dangerous hours left in service. What a royal mess.

No wonder Jose declined the request of changing the existing bus to a bigger and better one. It was all about money not quality service.

The tension accelerated. Maritza gave us two choices:

1. Go to the Jewish Federation for a lecture and purchase lunch
2. Head back to the ship in Santos

Everyone wanted a chance to explore the immediate vicinity and at least have lunch at a local restaurant. This seemed to be a reasonable request.

Maritza adamantly said, "Definitely not, because we are in the highest crime area of São Paulo."

Most continued to loudly voice their opinions. Tensed, Maritza contacted the main office and told her boss (Francisco's colleague) about the defective situation.

Jose replied, "All the participants must go to the Federation for a lecture and purchase lunch. It has already been set up especially for the group. After lunch, they are scheduled to return back to the port."

I was faced with no choice but to make an immediate critical decision for the safety and well-being of the group. Of course, arriving back to the ship on time was a priority.

A late arrival meant that the group would be chasing the ship to her next port of call (a cruiser's disaster), so I announced, "There will be no visit to the Jewish Federation, nothing as such was mentioned in my itinerary or contract. The huge mistake emanated from two conflicting contracts and itineraries."

Regarding the food, which was especially prepared for the group, I hoped the Federation would donate it to those in need.

At this point, it was way past lunch time. Everyone felt hungry, angry, agitated, and pushed to their limits after sitting in the bus and van for much too long. If that wasn't enough misery, the heat and humidity didn't help. The air conditioner inside the ailing bus pretty much made noise and nothing else.

Not far from the two parked vehicles, Maritza spotted a gas station that seemed to be somewhat safe. She suggested purchasing snacks and using the restroom. The person who used the gas station's men's room later said that it was cleaner than the one on our bus. No wonder I didn't want to check it out.

Maritza then announced, "Since we're not stopping at the Federation, there's time to visit a famous coffee plantation not far from Santos. We'll stop there as the clock will permit."

Then I made a poetic announcement:

"This entire **day**,
Is a complete **decay**.
Due to some planners that are **liars**,
They organized a tour as if being **minors**.
For your most precious **time**,
None of you will pay a **dime**."

Before heading to the coffee plantation, some people wanted to swap vehicles. I accommodated all changes and ended up with the last seat on the sick bus. The driver started the engine, he succeeded but only after a few failed attempts. The traffic wasn't too bad, and Maritza was optimistic that a visit to the coffee plantation was still a go (something good on a bad day). For a change, I was a bit at ease, but not for very long.

Looking far into the horizon, I asked Maritza if we were approaching Santos.

She replied, "Yes. It's a city by the ocean, and soon, the waters of the Atlantic will appear."

Uh oh, traffic started escalating on the busy highway (and so did my nerves). The constant stop and go wasted our precious time and more stress on the ailing bus that seemed to be on its last leg. No sooner than later the bus stopped. Somehow, the driver barley maneuvered the failing machine to the shoulder of the highway. Thereafter it took a big choke, then flatlined, within a few seconds the bus died. We were all in shock and wondered what could possibly come next.

As a result of this new development, Maritza announced, "The coffee plantation is not an option anymore."

Good Lord, coffee was the last thing on my mind; staying alive in the middle of a major highway was the priority.

Soon, the driver of the van carefully stopped to assess what was going on, he couldn't help because his vehicle was full. So, the van's passengers were in awe while waving their goodbyes. Poor 30 of us. I was glad that Alex and Ruth were safe in the van.

We all evacuated the deceased bus onto a small grassy median of the congested main highway. The humidity and heat further aggravated our misery (more danger added to the crisis). Everyone was scared and humiliated standing between crowded traffic. I was on needles and pins, afraid we would not arrive back at the port on time, or not at all.

Maritza immediately called her idiotic boss (Jose) and frantically demanded a functional bus for the remaining portion of the drive to the ship. Time was crucial. We were still about 15 miles from the port, and the 6:00p.m. set sail was approaching (along with my next nervous breakdown). Maritza and I were beside ourselves. Feeling so bad for everyone, especially the elderly. I couldn't look at any of the group members, because if looks could kill, this would have been my final resting place, like the dead bus.

Slowly dying from anxiety while we waited for another bus to appear, I kept my eyes peeled in the dimming sunlight, wondering when we would be on our way back to the ship. Finally, a replacement bus showed up. With great relief, all of us quickly prepared to board the newer bus. More importantly, we had to be extremely careful from the fast-driving vehicles which were only a few feet from the 30 faultless and shaking passengers. It was just like a scene from a horror movie.

Minutes before 6:00p.m., we arrived at the port's terminal. My problems were not over just yet. It takes time to go through border control and security. Set sail was moments away.

Reminder: the ship is not obliged to wait a second after 6:01p.m. sharp, and not responsible for the late passengers' expenses in the event that anyone missed the ship and had to chase it at the next port of call.
End of reminder.

At that point and in a great hurry, I had to part from Maritza because only the ship's passengers were allowed to proceed.

I told her, "You were wonderful. Nothing was your fault. In the event I'll need your testimony for legal action, I'll get in touch with you. I have your business card."

She replied, "My boss and Francisco were totally wrong. They had two different contracts and itineraries. Whatever you need from me, I'll comply promptly."

As we hugged, Maritza gave me a note from her boss' stationary, detailing the failed day.

Passport control went smoothly and quickly because with the exception of Conny's group, every single passenger was already on board the ship, however, we were not out of the woods yet. Next came the security check. Luckily, that also went swiftly for the same reason.

With our hearts pounding and bolting at everyone's maximum capacity, all of us ran with lots of aching body parts to the dock, which I prayed was still open. By approximately 6:10p.m., all 30 shaking tourists, totally out of breath and filled with stress, stepped onto the delayed ship. Wonderful David waited and greeted an exhausted group of people with a sigh of relief. I almost collapsed when I saw him.

David said, "I know everything that happened and why you are the last to board, when some of your tour members arrived earlier, they informed me about the failed bus. Good thing you made it. I could only hold the ship for a few more minutes. It's totally against company policy to do what I did. My dear Conny, I am hoping not to face any consequences by detaining the ship for you after 6:01p.m."

It had been my most stressful day ever, but I counted my blessings that we were alive and spared from chasing the ship to her next port of call, which is a small island in one of the most remote areas of Brazil.

Note: How in the world was I supposed to do just that with 29 rightful complainers?

End of note.

Alex and Ruth anxiously awaited near the entryway. Of course, they'd been worried about the ones who were stranded in the median of a major highway. When they spotted me, I noticed the look of ease that had passed over both faces. Hugs then detoxing with steaming hot shower was urgently needed. This near-deadly day would not soon be forgotten.

Once recovery had somewhat set in, I went down to the tour desk and asked the manager, "Do you offer a one-day tour to both Santos and São Paulo?"

He replied, “Ma’am, it’s impossible to visit those two cities while the ship docks in Santos for merely ten hours.”

I replied while showing him the cruise’s itinerary and daily schedule, “It read and I quote, ‘Arriving São Paulo/ Santos 8:00a.m. Departing 6:00p.m.’” I told the manager that’s wrong, it should have stated, “Arriving Santos 8:00a.m., departing 6:00p.m. Santos is approximately 52 miles away from São Paulo and does not have a seaport. Attempting to visit both cities, while the ship is docked for only ten hours, is absolutely not recommended. Doing so is a sure risk, and the ship will not wait. The cruise line posting was wrong.” The manager agreed with me.

Why in the world would 40 people on a luxury vacation want to endure a lengthy drive, while sitting for hours in traffic, then be forced to attend a random lecture at a federation, and be forced to purchase lunch? How bad can bad be, being on an ailing bus full of innocent people all on a dangerous ride in the middle of a congested highway?

The sick bus should have been on its final drive to the junkyard and nowhere else.

I didn’t think that Jose, the “expert in tourism” (more like a rookie), would have a single answer. Francisco and him should not be selling tourism by all means.

It was a highly unsafe day for everyone as well as an expensive port for me. I could live with the expense but not the danger of a bus full of people.

I wouldn’t be surprised if some of the tour members had one of the hardest days in their lives.

Indeed, I did.

CHAPTER 26

"No" Is an Okay Answer

Friday, February 20, Ilhabela, Brazil

The ship will be docked from 7:00a.m. to 6:00p.m.

On a very small and pretty island.

The group members could do as they wish. Some options were taking a taxi to city center, roaming around the pier, perhaps just relaxing by the ship's pool. I desperately needed to unwind, surely some others wanted to do so, as well. The day before had been a killer.

Word got around the ship, that the Santos/São Paulo experience was completely bungled, thanks to Jose, who planned an impossible tour of two cities in one day and provided a nonfunctioning bus.

From this moment, I made a decision to cease all tag-alongs. Really, who would want any part of my tours at this point anyway? It wouldn't surprise me if no one from my group trusted Francisco's planning for the remaining three tours. Almost everything concerning him was negative, problematic, and troublesome.

Meanwhile, David recommended that we visit a nice private beach with calm waters. Alex, Ruth, and I elected to check it out and agreed to have lunch somewhere different from the ship's kitchen. Before the three of us went to the taxi stand, I asked David if he had any negative issues with his superiors about the late 'set sail' the day before.

He said, "All is well."

That's what I wanted to hear.

We arrived at the secluded cove. Our visit was relaxing at its best. I treasured every second of the easy and tranquil hours. What a difference from the previous day, full of stress and dangerous antics.

I spotted a mom-and-pop eatery, just what we wanted, a change from the food prepared by the ship's chefs. I especially enjoyed the hot and spicy dish. Ruth and Alex elected milder choices. It was a totally successful outing, thanks to David, he came to my rescue once again.

Upon returning to the ship, a nap was due. Ruth's cabin was next to us, which worked perfectly, because she was never alone for too long, at any given time.

At 5:00p.m., I fancied a hot drink, so Ruth and I went to the high tea concession. Two ladies sitting just adjacent to us spoke Hebrew. I couldn't help but hear them complain about the pricey tickets to Rio's Parade that the ship was offering. Waiting until they were done with their drink and snack, I very nicely approached and introduced myself. I told them, "I'm holding a few extra tickets that are $200 cheaper than the ship's."

The ladies were happy about the significant savings and said, "Allow us to consider your offer for a day or two. Please provide your room number, in the event we want to join your group, we'll touch base."

The next day, I met the ladies, and two of the Parade tickets were sold. They each gave me their business card, one was an artist, and the other, a lawyer. Both resided in

Tel-Aviv, Israel. I held on to the lawyer's business card (along with Maritza's). I also invited them to meet my group at the Shabbat Eve worship services. Why not? There's lots of common ground with the Hebrew speaking circle of people.

David and the ladies joined along with other Jewish passengers. It was the first time I had seen a need for more chairs at a Friday night service, on the high seas. The evening continued as planned.

After all the activities, I called David and said, "Can you meet me in the buffet at 10:00p.m.? There's a sensitive and important question I want to ask you." He agreed and we met on time.

Before asking him my question, I said, "'No is an okay answer." After a deep breath, I started with a gray lie, "For my wonderful group, would it be possible to have a tour of the bridge?"

Note: The bridge room is similar to the cockpit on an airplane, and it's always kept under tight security.
End of note.

He looked at me with a strange expression and said, "My dear Conny, you're a travel agent and should know better, securities around the world drastically changed, therefore, tours to the bridge had been suspended."

How well I knew that, but it's not a sin to ask. He quietly thought for a few seconds, and I started to feel a bit like a fool.

He then said, "Let me get back to you after speaking to my superior."

I gave him the biggest smile together with a hug and said, "Thank you for your consideration by trying and Shabbat Shalom."

I never ceased to do the utmost for the benefit of my groups. I've seen the bridge several times before, and it was an extremely interesting experience. While waiting anxiously for David's answer, I prepared myself for a 'no' response. Good night to another pleasurable day, without Francisco.

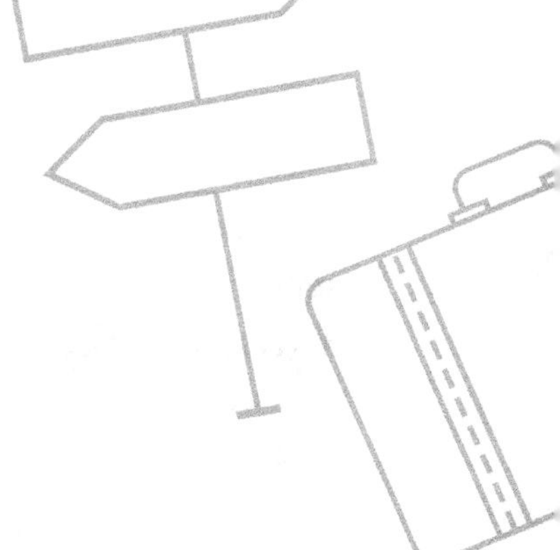

CHAPTER 27

A Gift for David

Saturday, February 21, Buzios, Brazil

THE SHIP WILL BE DOCKED from 7:00a.m. to 6:00p.m.

The schedule is pretty much as the day before. I loved having two consecutive free days.

Just as the three of us went to breakfast, David called and announced, "The captain has made a one-time exception, allowing your group a visit to the bridge."

I questioned my hearing and said, "I misheard you, please repeat yourself."

The second time seemed like music to my ears. I was elated!

He further said, "Please tell your group, not a word to anyone onboard the ship about the bridge tour. I will also need everyone's passport for security check, so kindly have them ready as soon as possible. The only time available to accommodate your special request will be in four days, while the ship is at sea."

I answered, "I'll adhere to all your instructions, and can't thank you enough."

He replied, "Glad to help. It's my pleasure."

That morning, I approached everyone and told them I needed their passports for a few hours. I was asked, by a few tour members why?

Quick thinking, I replied, "for re-entering Brazil."

A white lie to keep the bridge tour, hush, hush, was my best bet. At that moment I decided to surprise the group and say nothing about the bridge tour. Therefore, it will be a sure well-kept secret.

Regarding yesterday's sale of the two Rio Parade tickets, I came across another chance to re-sell the remaining six on board the ship.

In fact, one more person asked me if I had another ticket, I answered "Unfortunately, I do not."

I was sorry to decline, but delighted and relieved that I kept my promise to the ones who had canceled the trip, thus salvaging them hundreds of dollars from the non-refundable Parade tickets.

Note: Upon arriving home, the first on my to-do list will be sending the checks to the four lucky couples who'd canceled.

End of note.

During this free day, my husband, Ruth, and I took a few hours to explore the city. I was so happy with David's good news that I almost danced my way as we exited the ship.

The little island was delightful and offered us a chance to buy some knickknacks. I was in search of a gift for David, but nothing caught my eye. The ship had a souvenir shop, so I planned to check it out.

Before going to dinner, I walked into the gift shop and immediately spotted a statuette replica of our ship. It even had its name engraved on it. I thought, bingo, this is for David. If he wanted a memento of the ship where he worked so diligently to secure everyone's safety, he would appreciate this appropriate and humble gift. That was the least I could do for the most wonderful person onboard the ship. I also purchased a thank you card for everyone to sign at our shalom (goodbye, in Hebrew) gathering with the superb, amazing, and deserving David.

At our next gathering, I showed the group David's gift that would be from all of us. The civil group members (about half of the group) complimented me on the gesture and asked if they could share the cost.

I said, "No, thank you."

CHAPTER 28

Rio, Rio, Rio de Janeiro

Sunday, February 22, Rio de Janeiro, Brazil

The ship will be docked from 8:00a.m. to 6:00p.m. on February 24 (three full days).

I'll quote the tour contract between Francisco and me, "A tour of Rio de Janeiro, 10:30a.m. to 5:00p.m. We will see the different neighborhoods of Rio. A visit to Corcovado. The fee for the train ride. Lunch is not included."

I woke up to a beautiful morning. The highlight of the trip is a mere day and a half away. We would soon be enjoying the world's most-watched Parade, known as the Rolls-Royce of them all, Rio Carnival Parade.

Stepping out onto my balcony, I saw Corcovado, the famous statue of Jesus Christ extending his arms as if he's embracing the amazing city. The clarity of the gorgeous blue skies and favorable weather exposed this massive world-renowned monument, an outstanding landmark, and a true signature of Brazil. If you haven't seen Corcovado from a distance, you haven't been to Rio de Janeiro.

I wondered what level of service we were to face with Francisco guiding us. I'll just have to wait and see, was I happy about this reunion? Not at all. My patience and of course loyalty had been completely depleted. I covered all of his mistakes thus far and there was no more room in my nervous system for his misguiding. How did the group feel about the reunion? Well, they hadn't forgotten the risky experience three days ago in São Paulo. Anxiously, I waited to see how many tour members would take Francisco's fifth tour. Soon I'll have a count. Surprisingly, more members came than I'd anticipated.

Once I spotted him, he welcomed us to Rio de Janeiro.

Again, he said, "I've been to this city, and seen the spectacular Parade 16 times in the last 16 years."

I was sick and tired hearing this quote over and again.

Oh, and by the way, of course Francisco had brought along another friend. He was introduced as an assistant. Yeah, right. We boarded the bus, which thank the Lord was nothing like the junky piece of machinery in Santos.

The first stop was a poverty-stricken area. People of all ages begged for money. Some were very young, right down to toddler age. Luckily, I always carried bills in small denominations to give the ones who extended their hands. I actually came prepared with lots of single dollars, knowing that some tour members will constantly ask me for change from large bills. It made me feel as if I had a banker's roll as well.

The level of poverty that we'd witnessed was overwhelming, and several of the tour members were uncomfortable witnessing such hardship. Our hearts went out to the struggling locals. It was not a usual stop nor on the contract.

We then continued on to an area where some of the flamboyant Parade floats were stationed for last-minute touch-ups before the upcoming event. Looking at them, I thought, No wonder it's a world-renowned Parade.

We had lunch at a famous hotel across from Copacabana Beach. Francisco allotted an hour to roam around and explore the world's sexiest beach. We saw lots of Itsy-bitsy, teeny-weeny (all colors) polka dot bikinis. Most were made of mere strings, no matter the size or shape of the wearer. Such a vision would prompt plenty of post trip conversations!

The next scheduled visit was to Corcovado. When we stopped at the gate to purchase tickets for the train ride up the mountain, the line of people looked as though it was a mile long. Of course the lengthy wait, it's during the yearly Parade. The dizzy guide that claimed to have visited Rio de Janeiro 16 times, didn't know that tickets could have been purchased hours in advance. His assistant should have waited in line to buy them during lunch or before. I supposed that dining out and impressing his assistant was more important than helping the group. (Some assistant). It surely seemed that Francisco's social life was more important than any consequences it may cause to his clients.

Finally, the tickets were purchased. Uh oh, unfortunately, here comes another major screwup:

We had to wait over an hour for our turn on the train. The group was annoyed and agitated again (rightfully so). Waiting in the heat, humidity, and direct sun was torture.

Wanting to get away from Francisco, I spotted a playground nearby. It had slides, swings, and some shade. Before taking advantage of the apparatuses, I invited the group to join me, making sure they all stayed away from the scorching sun. There was never a dull moment with this narcissistic guide. Another bus tour to be discounted.

Finally, it was our turn to board the train up to Corcovado. What an extraordinarily huge and mind-boggling monument. The scenery atop the mountain was second to none from all angles. No postcard or professional photograph could replicate the 360-degree view of the city, beaches, ocean, and mountains from the height of this massive statue. If you haven't been to the top of Corcovado, you haven't been to Rio de Janeiro.

Most of the group members didn't want to move on, even after a good hour plus. No one could get enough of Brazil's signature treasure.

On the bus, while driving back to the ship, Francisco announced, "Tonight is the biggest pre-party celebrating Rio Carnival Parade. It takes place at the famous Copacabana Beach! Anyone wants to join me or team up? It's an amazing all-night party."

Was he kidding? No one seemed interested. It was definitely an event for the young and young at heart.

Before we exited the bus to board the ship, Francisco said, "Tomorrow, after our morning half-day tour, a rest is advised because the Parade will continue until the wee hours of the morning."

Again, he repeated he'd been to 16 Rio Carnival Parades in the last 16 years. Hopefully, it would be the last time that I'd hear that tune. So, onto the ship we proceeded. For Francisco, the Copacabana all-night beach party was not to be missed. Where and how in the world would he accumulate the energy and strength, while he just guided us on an all-day tour and the following:

1. He's planning to join the opening party of Rio's Parade, which would continue until the early hours. (The next day)
2. A few hours later, Francisco is scheduled to guide us on a tour to Sugarloaf Mountain.
3. Then get ready for Rio Carnival Parade.
4. In the evening a transfer to the Parade's stadium. Another all-night event.

These factors and crazy planning add up to 48 sleepless hours. I hoped this grueling schedule would not result in more mishaps and mistakes. Wishful thinking.

After dinner, the ship had Brazilian entertainment, including traditional music and dancers. The talented performances with their sexy high heels encouraged the passengers to join the dancing. Soon, lots of the ship's travelers were immersed with learning the Samba and the floor rocked the night away.

Before retiring for the night, I reminded the group about having a goodnight's sleep because the following day would be the busiest and longest of the trip. Unfortunately, Francisco didn't practice what he preached.

CHAPTER 29

The Worst Transfer to the Best Parade

Monday, February 23

RIO DE JANEIRO, BRAZIL: SECOND full day.

The tour contract between Francisco and me stated, Half-day tour to Sugarloaf Mountain from 9:00a.m. to 2:00p.m. In the evening hours, a round trip transfer from the ship to Rio Carnival Parade's stadium will be provided.

On a timely manner, as scheduled, the bus arrived. Francisco totally looked like a zombie and could not stop yawning. I had the feeling that we would have to deal with a sleep-deprived guide who could possibly be prone to making more and greater mistakes. I feared that it would spill over to the most important event (coming up in less than 11 hours). Apprehension gripped my nerves because I had no way of knowing what's next due to Francisco's exhausted state of mind.

We all boarded the bus heading to Sugarloaf Mountain. Rio de Janeiro is not a big city, and within a short while, we arrived at our destination. The looming peak was given that name because it looked like a stick of sugar cane.

Francisco asked me to buy the lift tickets, which I did. Soon, we were riding the cable car and on our way to the top of the mountain. Once there, I realized that we could have forfeited the ride to the top of Sugarloaf Mountain because the view is exactly the same as Corcovado Mountain, which we toured yesterday for over two hours.

Francisco should have advised us to share taxis and be dropped off at the base (bottom) of Sugarloaf Mountain. The scenery from the flats is the main feature, it's breath-taking and not to be missed. He also should have told us to have a break in a local brewery or one of the cafes facing the stunning and unique mountain. This arrangement would have been much more practical for the group as well as the dizzy guide. Francisco could have utilized those precious morning hours to catch up on his sleep from the all-night Copacabana beach party, but he was not capable of making the right decisions for all concerned.

After the unnecessary and repetitious tour, while driving back to the port, Francisco announced, "I am picking you up at 8:00p.m. sharp. We will have plenty of time, since the Parade begins at 9:00p.m."

Half of the group protested, wanting to be picked up earlier. Francisco announced again, "I know what I am doing 8:00p.m. is appropriate. I've been attending Rio's Parade for the last 16 years, so, 8:00p.m. is correct."

Shlomo the dictator favored the lousy guide's 8:00p.m. pickup. I was sure that he and Sharon did not want to miss a dinner onboard the ship. Such a dumb excuse! However, with some persuading, the weak tour members changed their mind and the vote of the 8:00p.m. transfer to the Parade prevailed.

At approximately 2:00p.m., we arrived at the port.

After everyone exited the bus, I told Francisco, "Please give me the Parade tickets."

He did. I stayed behind to count them, making sure that I had the correct amount. I did.

Just before heading to the ship, Francisco told me, "Please, please, please, Conny, don't tell anyone, but one of your tour members asked me this morning where and how to locate an orgy?"

I immediately said, "I do not want to know who." I wasn't sure what to think (it hit me like a rock), but if true, this personal information was none of my business. Francisco had violated that person's confidence by repeating a personal issue. It was the second time he repeated a conversation that was meant for his ears only. The first time was in Buenos Aires, with an issue of Hellen's $20.

Meanwhile, there went my appetite for lunch.

When I entered the ship's lobby, many people were forming a long line.

I asked a crew member what was going on. I was told, "The passengers who bought the Parade tickets from the ship are getting ready to queue up for the buses and transfer to the Parade's stadium. Doors open at 5:00p.m., and at that time, thousands of people will storm into the 'first come, first served' section seven, to secure seating space on the benches."

Our tickets were for the same location as the ship's Parade package. Francisco's transfer was scheduled for 8:00p.m., six hours from now, and the passengers from the ship were getting ready for the transfer. I was livid.

A feeling started brewing that the crescendo was about to be a calamity.

My stress level went haywire, to say the least. Francisco had 16 years' experience and here was another major screwup in the making. I immediately called him to change the pickup time, but no answer to any of my many attempts. Of course, he didn't pick up the phone. The tired guide was sleeping on our time. He had two days of consecutive touring and an all-night party in between, which would drag anyone into deep hibernation. It was none of my business what Francisco did with his free time (I would not begrudge anyone a party), but it was surely my business what he's doing on our precious hours, for which he was paid handsomely many months in advance.

I grabbed a seat and started thinking how to rectify the situation. I quickly came to the conclusion that an emergency meeting at the buffet was imperative. At once, I reached out to each tour member and those who bought the eight extra tickets. All arrived promptly. Before starting to speak, I handed each person their Parade ticket. I then started the meeting. Without exception, all had an opinion about Francisco's 8:00p.m. pickup time. The entire group yelled and couldn't come to a common-ground resolution. Another situation in disarray! A smaller version of the tumultuous scene in São Paulo.

Out of the eight resold tickets, four were sold to Americans, they stood up and said, "This unruly commotion is not for us. We are taking a taxi on our own to the stadium." Hooray for them.

The other four tickets had been sold to Israelis. They elected to stay at the chaotic meeting. Now, the group of 34 shrunk by four, the new count, 30 Parade goers.

I then took a deep breath and demanded that everyone pay attention to me. Surprisingly, they did, including Shlomo, the one who dictated the 8:00p.m. transfer.

I told them, "I was just advised, by the ship's tour desk, that 8:00p.m. is absolutely very late to leave for the Parade. "As I am speaking, all of the passengers who purchased Parade tickets directly from the ship, and in the same section as us, are lining up and boarding the buses for the transfer to the stadium. I called Francisco several times to inform him that 8:00p.m. is not acceptable, and we must change the pickup time. Unfortunately, he didn't answer any of my calls. Surely, he's making up sleep after being awake for 48 straight hours." I adamantly announced to the group, "An 8:00p.m. departure to the Parade is extremely late, and a big mistake is in the making. So here are my correct instructions:

1. Team up or proceed on your own as soon as possible
2. Wait at the pier's taxi stand for a ride to the stadium
3. Advise the driver to drop you off at section seven

I will reimburse all taxi fares. Raise your hands if you understand and agree."

Excluding Shlomo, the dictator and his wife, everyone favored my correct instructions.

While all hands were still in the air, Shlomo stood up, pointed his index finger at the entire group, and loudly said, "I want to see, I want to see, who is not following Francisco's instructions?"

Within a heartbeat, all hands dropped even though less than a few seconds earlier, everyone agreed to take my correct directions. The entire group changed their minds. Nobody challenged the monstrous bully, so 8:00p.m. prevailed. I couldn't believe my eyes and ears. How weak the tour members were, by obeying Shlomo's militant behavior. The dictator ruled the jungle. His bullying was a threat to the group.

This is where and when I reached a tipping point. My stress level was severely elevated that it caused me to have a complete blackout. From this moment and until weeks after the trip, I had zero recollection of:

1. The 8:00p.m. transfer to the Parade is extremely late
2. I warned the entire group that this was another huge mistake from Francisco
3. I gave everyone correct instructions regarding when and how to arrive at the Parade on time and in dignity

Happily, Shlomo announced that he'd see everyone at 8:00p.m. All drifted away and went about their business. At approximately 6:00p.m., coincidentally, I passed through the nearly empty dining room and spotted only Sholomo and Sharon calmly stuffing their faces. Heaven forbid they would miss a free dinner on the ship, instead of being at the Parade stadium, where thousands of visitors were already securing their viewing space. Conny's group was the exception, still on board the ship with no sign of being on our way to the Parade, the theme and reason for the entire trip.

Below is some brief information regarding Rio Carnival Parade:

- The stadium has a total of 13 sections
- The first two are occupied by locals (these are the least desirable and most cost-efficient seats)
- The rest of the sections are for visitors and tourists (they have better viewing, but progressively get pricier)
- Section seven is a very popular location due to its exceptional view. However, it offers only space on the concrete benches (available on a first come, first served basis)
- Bringing a cushion is recommended, or spectators can rent one
- Rio Carnival Parade is based on the performances of nine samba schools from Brazil only. Each year, before the Parade, all schools are ranked by professional judges on their performances using several parameters: dancing, choreography, synchronization, flamboyant costumes and floats, as well as exuberant music

The nine schools are separated into three categories:

1. Category A, ranked excellent. Those schools performed (second in line) at prime time, which is mid-Parade.

2. Category B, ranked very good. Those schools performed (first in line) before prime time; they are the opening act.
3. Category C, ranked good. Those schools performed (third in line) after prime time; they concluded the Parade.

Each of the schools had about eight flamboyant floats and some marching bands sprinkled in between.

All schools had an equal allotted time for their performances (about forty minutes). Occasionally, a cleanup crew comes through to pick up the flying debris from the floats. This created approximately a 20-minute break in between performances, and for the standing spectators with sitting space on the concrete benches (which was section seven), it was an opportunity to sit down.

End of briefing.

By 8:00p.m., all 30 of us waited for Francisco and the bus at the same location where he had dropped us earlier. Because that evening was the last time we'd see Francisco, five couples gave me an envelope containing his tips. The ones who tipped Francisco were Jack and Jacqueline, Pete and Kiti, Mr. and Mrs. Goldfinger, Sam and Samantha, as well as Shlomo and Sharon.

I wished that they had not given the envelopes to me, but rejection is not nice, so I put them in my fanny pack for later delivery. Out of 26 people in the group, only ten tipped him. Hellen noticed and figured out what's going on with the envelopes, so she was the first one shouting loud and clear, "No tip for Francisco from me." Some other tour members had no problem quietly agreeing.

By 8:05p.m., no Francisco or bus in sight. All of us were aggravated and anxious to be in the Parade's stadium. I asked a taxi driver what's the distance to the stadium. Despite him speaking very little English, I understood that it was approximately four miles from the ship.

At 8:10p.m. The same nerve-racking status.

By 8:15p.m., tension grew by the second. Obviously, because of my blackout, I didn't remind the group that I'd warned them and provided clear instructions on when and how to arrive at the stadium on time.

At 8:20p.m., Sally, Hellen, Matilda, Solomon, and Sue no longer wanted to wait. The wise five took a taxi to the Parade. They followed my directions a little late, but better than never. Our group shrunk by five, and the new count was 25 nervous, late Parade goers.

I announced again, "Take a taxi to the stadium, and I will reimburse you."

No one followed my directions. Though I wanted to grab a cab for Alex, Ruth, and me but I didn't. This would not be right because it's my duty to stay with the remaining stubborn tour members.

By 8:25p.m., the later-than-late bus finally arrived. Francisco jumped out all hyped up, totally disoriented, and completely confused, spouting excuses about traffic. Of course, there was traffic! Rio was having its major international annual event! The city was saturated with what seemed to be millions of people who came to view the most famous Parade in the world.

Since this was Francisco's 17th time in 17 years, he definitely should have known that there would be heavy traffic in the midst of Rio de Janeiro on the evening of the most popular Parade.

While one by one, the nervous and upset members anxiously boarded the bus.

I quickly took Francisco aside and angrily told him, "You claimed over and again that you have been to 16 Rio Carnival Parades in the last 16 years. Shouldn't you have known that there would be traffic on the evening of the most popular Parade in the world?"

He had no answer, not even a lie. As my anger escalated, I continued, "The passengers who bought tickets to the Parade from the ship, started lining up about six hours ago."

Again, he said, "There was traffic." Obviously, the liar did what liars do and continued to lie.

I further said, "I know the reason you are late. It's because you've been sleeping on our time due to over-exerting yourself for two straight days. In addition, last night's party caused you to have 48 sleepless hours. Instead of the unnecessary tour to Sugarloaf Mountain you should have utilized some of those precious hours catching up on your sleep. The group could have gone by taxis to that most unique mountain, which viewing it from the flats is preferable over taking the cable car up to see a repetitious view."

He had no reply. This was the hallmark behavior of an irresponsible person.

Francisco and I boarded the bus last. Before sitting down, I tossed him his five envelopes in disgust and later regretted having done so.

As we were on our way, I couldn't understand why the driver circled the same area over and again. The port was approximately four miles away from the stadium.

Lo and behold, the bus came to a complete stop. The driver found a dingy spot in a dark alley. We all exited the bus in the middle of nowhere and wondered where in the world Francisco was taking us.

Close to 9:00p.m., The group began to walk. The Parade was scheduled to start within a few minutes.

Still leading us along the most poorly paved walkway I'd ever seen, it started to get dark. Most of us struggled with every step, so we held each other to avoid falling (that's all I needed, someone to break a bone), we continued.

A minute after 9:00p.m., the enormous lights and extremely loud opening music was a clear indication that the Parade started. I hoped that the stadium would soon come into view at any moment, but no such luck. The struggle must go on, thanks to Francisco and Shlomo. Making matters worse, the humidity added to our misery.

The ones with health issues were starting to wear out. No one could have predicted this treacherous transfer. I was afraid another migraine would creep into my head, but I tried my best to ignore those thoughts and focus on the group's safety, which was a priority, all while wishing I'd wake up from this nightmare.

Somehow, the 25 of us arrived at the main intersection, but still no stadium in sight.

Since the enormous number of pedestrians and the overflow of visitors in Rio de Janeiro throughout the week, the city had assembled a huge temporary suspension bridge. Did we have to climb it? Sure, why not? Now we found ourselves ascending many steps towards the top of the bridge. My cute little stepmom needed assistance to climb, so I positioned her under my arm and held on to her for dear life. All the ones who were well enough aided those who were not. Amazing Pete helped Kiti's old uncle. He should have been looking for an assisted living facility, not suffering through Francisco's impossible guiding. Everyone was worn out, and some were on the verge of giving up, but we had to climb the stairs, no other choice. My nightmare continued, as we followed the moron who had been to 16 Rio Carnival Parades, in the last 16 years.

Finally, all of us reached the top of the bridge. Surprise, it was swaying. A main and busy boulevard bloomed hundreds of feet below, as the rocking and rolling bridge continued to move. Walking to the other end of the dancing bridge was extremely scary. The same number of steps we had ascended, of course, needed to descend. Aside from being drained, each one started slowly down the stairs to the bottom of the swinging bridge. Perhaps after this doomed trip, some knee replacements would be necessary.

Upon landing at street level and still no sign of the stadium we approached a hilly Street. I prayed that there was no need to climb it, but why not? Once again, my prayers were not answered. Begrudgingly, the group trudged along like a herd of mountain goats hiking up a hill.

By now, Sam and Samantha, Jack, and Jacqueline, Goldfinger and his wife were limping so pronouncedly that they were in no way able to continue the hazardous transfer. Minutes later, the three couples took taxis back to the ship. What a shame, they should have listened to me and taken a taxi to the stadium hours ago. The group shrunk by six, last count, 19 exhausted Parade goers.

Once we reached the top of the hill, Francisco told us that the stadium was a short distance away, but he forgot to say there was still more ground to cover.

At approximately 10:00p.m., at last, the 19 of us reached the last upper entrance of section seven and tickets were checked for entry. At this point, the lying guide was nowhere to be seen. He'd abandoned us, probably to a better section with his friends. After all, that was his 17th time in 17 years enjoying the world-famous Parade. More unprofessional behavior from the unprofessional guide.

Just as one of the doors to section seven opened, all of us were dumbfounded to suddenly be part of a wall-to-wall mass of people. We couldn't believe our eyes and were trying to control the racing heartbeats that made the nervous system almost shutter. Without exaggeration, it felt like being thrown into a tin can of sardines.

The graduated aisles that separated the concrete benches did not have an inch to spare. Bodies and more bodies pressed together. We were anchored at the top of the stairs with no room for the slightest movement. Anyone of average height or shorter could only hear the music (which was so loud, it could have awakened the dead), and forget about seeing any fraction of the floats. For the tall individuals, an obstructed view of the fascinating floats seemed somewhat possible, but still an unbearable situation. For this luxury, we'd each paid $450.

The graduated steps between the benches were overflowing with spectators from top to bottom. No one sat, everybody stood in order to see the floats. When the cleanup crew came to do their chores, it was the only time that the lucky ones, with bench space, had a chance to sit and take the load off their feet. All others, including the 19 of us, continued to stand on the aisle steps in an awkward position while suffering from aches and pains. After the cleanup, the floats resumed to perform and section seven continued with its madness. Though it was a frightening situation, we had no choice, because there were no other options.

Midnight rolled around, it had been over two hours of agony. The people without bench space were still standing motionless the entire time. What a delightful torture, with no end in sight.

Just before 1:30a.m., I noticed that some people were slowly vacating the benches. It made sense, because they were the ones who had entered the stadium at approximately 5:00p.m. (when the doors opened) to secure space per the instructions of their professional tour guides, unlike our unprofessional guide. They'd been able to view the first and second schools, ranking excellent and very good, but now, they were probably beyond pleasant exhaustion.

This welcome process decreased the number of spectators and enabled the ones who had been standing on the aisles for hours to finally sit down and view the Parade, but only spectating the schools that ranked good (Category C). We totally missed the schools that ranked excellent and very good (Category A and B).

It wasn't long before our eyes started to droop. Though we had arrived at the stadium around 10:00p.m., the extreme agony of the lengthy transfer was beyond exhausting to everyone's capacity.

By 2:30a.m., while sitting with fully droopy eyes, and yawning nonstop, the group determined that it was useless to remain in the stadium. Our tired bodies clocks could no longer tick.

At this time one or two floats still remained to be viewed, with significantly smaller audience. While wobbling out of the stadium, I spotted our driver, who'd managed to reposition the bus and park it closer to section seven. Some tour members elected to take a taxi, which I reimbursed later. The rest boarded the bus for the drive back to the ship. Francisco was nowhere in sight. In broken English, the driver told me that he would be coming any minute.

From the front row, where Shlomo and his wife always sat, he shouted, "I want my tip money back."

At that moment, I totally regretted giving Francisco the five envelopes. I should have held them so Shlomo could have his tip money returned and perhaps the other four couples, do as they wished.

Note: I quickly made the decision that I'd return Shlomo's $50 tip, via my checking account, because in the event that I'd face Francisco in court, my canceled check would be a prize-winning piece of evidence, regarding the guide's ailing leadership.

End of note.

Within a few minutes, the unprofessional guide arrived. Shlomo was so furious at him but kept his big mouth shut for a change. The others said nothing. We were all exhausted and rather not listen to Francisco's excuses, which would be lies from all directions.

It took the driver less than five minutes to arrive at the port.

While Shlomo exited the bus, Francisco said, "Goodbye Shlomo."

No response. The dictator truly despised the sight of the lousy guide and wanted nothing to do with him. The remaining few were silently on their way out the door. I too, turned from Francisco without offering a final farewell. Sometimes, silence says a lot.

While proceeding to the ship, one of the civil tour members put his arm around my shoulders and said, "Conny, during our walk in the dark alley, Francisco told me that you refused to pay $50 to park the bus."

I responded, "What a liar! The Parade tickets, transfer, and parking fee were all included. Everything was paid for in full before the trip. When we get together tonight, I'll show you the receipt." I further stated, "If Francisco had asked me to pay it again, I would have done so in a heartbeat."

As I entered the ship, I spotted the five who took a taxi to the stadium at 8:30p.m. Sally, Hellen, Matilda, Solomon, and Sue all seemed happy and content.

I asked, "Where were you all night long? Your absence worried me."

Solomon answered, "The taxi driver took us to a section with front-row seats."

I further asked, "Seats or concrete benches?

"He replied, "Very comfortable seats."

I wondered if they had slipped the taxi driver, or a Parade employee some money, in order to have better seating. With money, one can buy their heart's desire, not just an upgraded seats at Rio's Parade. I did not ask, better not to know.

Fast forward: two weeks post trip, I called the headquarters of the Parade in Rio de Janeiro and spoke with a manager.

I asked him, "How many people, in total, can sit comfortably on the concrete benches in section seven, and still view the Parade?"

I was told 7,500.

I replied, "On February 23, without exaggeration, at least twice as many people were crammed into section seven. The aisles were so crowded with spectators, there was no more room for another person to stand between the concrete seats from the top to the bottom of the stairs."

His only comment was, "That's why we tell people to arrive as early as they can."

End of fast forward.

It didn't take a genius putting two and two together. Why had Rio Carnival Parade's management allowed more than double the capacity of spectators in section seven? Greed and corruption can be offensive. At least, for a worldly event, a safer and stronger code should be enforced.

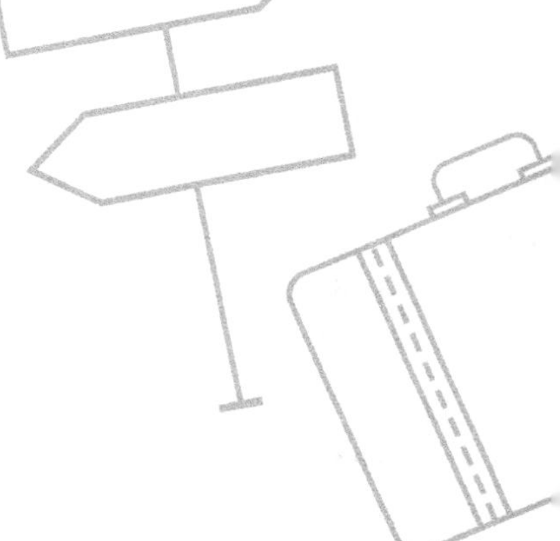

CHAPTER 30

Arrivederci, Rio

TUESDAY, FEBRUARY 24, RIO DE Janeiro, Brazil.

The third and final full day. The ship will sail at 7:00p.m.

With the exception of the staff and I, there wasn't a single person roaming around in the early morning hours. Probably everyone on the entire ship was sound asleep, being exhausted from the nightly one-of-a-kind Parade. I ventured to say that the only cruise passengers not at Rio's Parade were the three couples from Conny's group. I felt terrible that they missed the headlining event. However, due to my loss of memory I couldn't tell them that it was their fault by not following my correct instructions, how and when to arrive at the Parade's stadium.

I couldn't believe that this was Francisco's 17th Parade. He performed like a Martian straight from Mars planning a trip to one of the greatest shows on earth for the first time. Now for the second time, he was responsible for exposing my group to danger and hardship. What good had he been since Punta del Este? None.

My stress level was overwhelming and devastation plagued me once again from Francisco's huge and harmful mistakes. It all ended up causing me another severe migraine. How much suffering can I endure on a trip that should have been pleasurable? Some tranquil time from this journey seemed to be many dreams away.

How could I ever face the group's complaints? Being still deep in my memory blackout and I blamed myself for the failed Parade viewing. With all that in mind, it made me a bit hungry, so I went to the buffet. As I entered Jack the jerk spotted and approached me. There went my appetite. He was one of the six that totally missed the Parade because of the exhausting and defective transfer, the three couples took taxis back to the ship.

Jack opened his big mouth with a question, "Conny, where did you purchase the Parade tickets?"

Being truthful as always, I answered, "From Francisco, who else do you think?"

I waited for an answer, he had none.

I continued, "I have the receipt in my cabin would you like to see it? Furthermore, Francisco told me many times that Rio Carnival Parade is owned and managed by a mafia." He said nothing.

I couldn't stand the sight of him for another second, so, withdrawing myself from his whereabouts was the best thing to do. I quickly grabbed some food then proceeded to my cabin.

Note: Regardless of whether or not the Parade was owned or managed by a mafia organization, Francisco should have known how to lead tourists on time and without causing aches and pains. I guess 16 Rio Parades were not enough to learn the proper arrival procedure. The group at large suffered and my list of problems saw no end from a guide named Francisco.

End of note.

I had a strong feeling that the minute Jack would see Shlomo and Sharon he'd tell them all about our conversation and for sure would add some lies.

For the rest of the day everyone did as they wished.

At 7:00p.m., the ship set sail, concluding her lengthy three-day stop in Rio de Janeiro. No need to tolerate Francisco's lying face anymore. I hoped this didn't run in the family because his cousin would be our guide at the last stop, Montevideo, Uruguay in two days.

After dinner and the evening activities, I planned another celebration. It was Mr. Cogan's 60th birthday. Like the other occasions, we signed the birthday card and presented a humble gift. Mr. Cogan expressed his gratitude, and the appreciation was welcome. Before adjourning for the night, I informed the group about two important events taking place the following day at sea:

1. "We will meet David at our designated gathering place, 10:30a.m. sharp. Everyone, please be on time. I suggest bringing cameras for a very special experience." Most wondered what it could be, but I left the bridge tour as a surprise, stating only, "Do not miss this interesting gathering." Jack told me he didn't want to join us, I said, "Do as you wish." I was thrilled.
2. "Since the beginning of the cruise, all of us have not dined together for an evening meal. I decided to make a pleasant change, and hoped everyone would enjoy. Let's wine and dine as a group tomorrow night, I'm hosting a dinner in the French restaurant at 7:00p.m. Anyone not wishing to

attend, please let me know soon." Of course, I was hoping that some tour members would decline the eloquent and expensive invitation. Wishful thinking.

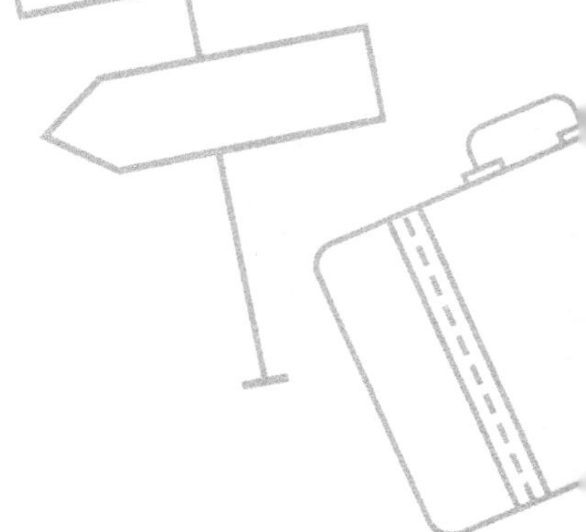

CHAPTER 31

One Busy Day

Wednesday, February 25

A DAY AT SEA, SOMEWHERE in the Atlantic Ocean.

At 10:30a.m., we congregated at our usual meeting place. Surprisingly, all were on time (with the exception of Jack and his poor wife). When David arrived, everyone welcomed him with a smile. He deserved the world from every tour member, but smiles, ear to ear, would do for the time being.

Due to strict security codes in the bridge, my group needed to be informed about some protocols and acceptable behavior. By doing so, the surprise was revealed earlier than anticipated, but all were delighted just as well.

We followed David through the staff-only corridors and soon arrived at a door requiring a secret code to unlock. All of us entered the controlled area of the ship with enthusiasm and curiosity. What an honor to be invited into the captain's territory. It was overwhelming to me that because of my chutzpah, the group was granted a very rare opportunity that is not normally available to the public due to security measures.

After we shook hands and took pictures with the master of the ship, he was called to attend other duties, so the captain introduced the chief engineer to us for our private tour. Wow, what a distinguished and dignified officer.

He greeted us by saying, "Welcome, everyone. It's my pleasure to brief you on this beautiful vessel. My name is Hans, and I come from Norway."

First, we saw the bow (which is the very front portion of the ship). It was a stunning view of the waves cascading just a few feet in front of us, truly a site to see above the deep ocean. We then continued to other sections of the bridge.

I noticed that all tour members gave Hans their undivided attention. Frankly, everyone couldn't get enough of Hans' impressive and informative presentation, delivered with lots of expertise and patience. If that wasn't enough, he encouraged us to sit on the captain's chair. Eagerly, each one did, and lots of photos were taken.

Thereafter, Hans extended his precious time by offering to have a question-and-answer session. The inquiries were many. I was so delighted to see everyone having an exceptional time, all thanks to David for making this private tour happen. This experience was not to be forgotten.

Before we began to disperse, I quickly reminded everyone to meet me in front of the French restaurant at 7:00p.m. sharp.

As we exited the bridge, every single person thanked the chief engineer. Even those who didn't appreciate anything, surprisingly expressed gratitude for this exquisite tour. David waited to escort us out of the bridge area to the public section.

I gave him a big hug and said, "Thank you ever so much."

Out of all people who's the one that stood right in front of us as we parted ways? It was none other than Jack. The group members elaborated to him how great the private visit to the bridge had been, and emphasized that he had missed one of the greatest moments onboard the ship. I witnessed Jack's disappointed look, for sure he knew he'd cut off his own nose to spite his face, it looked as if he regretted missing my add-on, which was a hit.

Lunch time approached, some members rushed to eat, Ruth and I went to play bingo. Yay, we won over $300, and then went for a slice of pizza, my favorite, followed by a fiesta for the long evening.

At 6:30p.m., I went to the restaurant before the group's arrival. It was important for me to inform the head waiter regarding wine consumption.

I said, "Each person should be offered one glass only. If anyone wanted a second serving, it would be okay with me."

I tried to be diplomatic by not dictating anything as such. Among the group, we already had one dictator, and it was one dictator too many.

I worried what Hellen's wild behavior had in mind for this evening. I will never forget the disgusting act she performed at the farm's zoo during the Punta del Este tour, when she picked up an hors d'oeuvre, took a bite, apparently not liking it, so she returned the uneaten portion back to the tray. (Even the monkey had more manners). Yes, she lacked every imaginable manner.

At 7:00p.m., the group started to arrive, all dressed nicely, and no one canceled. Darn it. For the second time, the table was set for 26 people in a U-shaped arrangement.

First in Buenos Aires at the restaurant for Shabbat Eve dinner, when Jack the jerk refused to pay $60 for his second plate.

While dining and socializing, I noticed that everyone enjoyed the get-together group dinner.

At the end of the wonderful meal filled with delicious food, wine, and mingling the waiter informed me, "Only a handful asked for more wine." I nodded and was pleasantly surprised.

As everyone started to disperse from the restaurant, I approached the three couples who totally missed Rio Carnival Parade, for a serious talk.

Important Note: At this point in time, I was still in my blackout and not remembering that I gave correct instructions of how to arrive at Parade's stadium on time.

End of note.

Aside from the following:

1. I wished that Jack and Jaqueline were not part of the group, I immensely disliked him, because he's selfish, uncultured, ungrateful, and a liar.
2. Life during the trip, would have been much sweeter without Goldfinger, it seemed as though he joined the group to show off his wealth which he never stopped talking about.
3. Sam and Samantha were nice (in comparison to their friends) but not nice enough to say, "Thank you," for collaborating his birthday event, two weeks ago.

With mixed feelings of annoyance and sympathy towards the three couples, I started the serious discussion and said, "I'm very sorry you missed the Parade. The mistakes were outrageous. I'm willing to reimburse you the $900 for two Parade tickets. I'll deal with my loss with Francisco after the trip."

The following were their answers:

1. Jack the jerk agreed to take the money. I told him I'd send a check after the trip.
2. Mr. Goldfinger, the millionaire, rudely said, "I don't need your money." I thought another jerk that I didn't bargain for.
3. Sam and Samantha very nicely said, "We don't want the refund." I was shocked and pleasantly surprised by the polite rejection of my generosity. At that very moment, I totally forgave Sam regarding the lack of appreciation for his birthday celebration.

Meanwhile, I couldn't understand the reason why Sam and Samantha rejected my generous offer. Could it be that they distinctly remembered the emergency meeting where I indeed warned the entire group of Francisco's extremely late transfer to the Parade, and I gave correct instructions regarding how and when to arrive at the Parade's stadium? Assuming my theory was correct (there was no other reason to reject my $900 refund), they probably figured out that no monies were due to anyone (Conny covered herself). How sad that neither one gave me a hint, if I was hinted about my correct instruction session to the Parade, perhaps my memory would have awoken right there and then, but nothing of the sort had happen. Very unfortunate for me.

When the evening's activities wrapped up and most adjourned to their cabins, I heard Hellen say, "Conny hosted the dinner because of all the mistakes she made." Her foul mouth, conniving personality, and rotten attitude fits the puzzle of a venomous being.

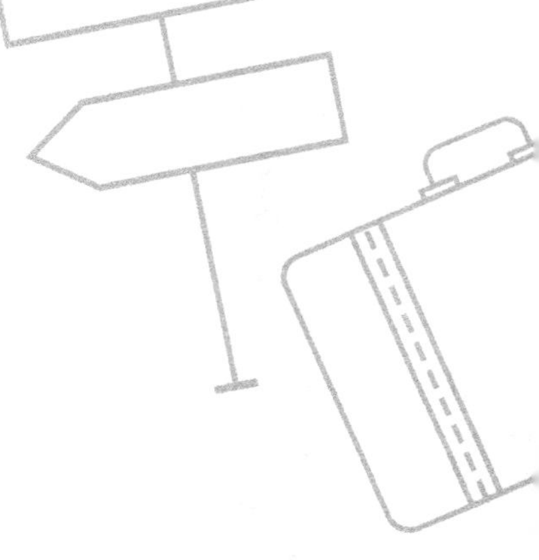

CHAPTER 32

It Could Have Been Better

Thursday, February 26, Montevideo, Uruguay

THE SHIP DOCKED FROM 7:00A.M. to 6:00p.m.

The tour contract planned by Francisco (his cousin would guide), you'll meet the guide at 9:00a.m. until 4:00p.m. Touring Montevideo including the Jewish sites. Lunch is included at a farm.

After breakfast, we met at our usual spot. I was really surprised to find more than half the group had waited for me. If I had a choice, I'd forfeit Francisco's final tour arrangement, but I didn't have that luxury.

We disembarked the ship and were on our way to locate the bus and guide. It didn't take long to spot each other. Leah, a young lady, welcomed us to her home city of Montevideo.

Not wanting another mistake, I insisted that we compare our contracts.

After reviewing them, Leah said, "Conny, according to your itinerary, we are supposed to visit the Jewish sites, but due to heightened security, we cannot. Francisco should've informed you of this situation."

I replied nonchalantly, "Francisco didn't know much of anything, especially guiding."

I had a feeling that Leah would transmit my words back to her cousin, but I couldn't care less. It was the truth. My tongue was ready to further tarnish her cousin's character but keeping matters to myself was the better choice. When I announced the news regarding the Jewish sites, the group was disappointed. Oh well, security supersedes.

Since a good portion of the tour was not possible, there wasn't much to see, except a drive through city center and visiting a leather factory with its retail shop. While browsing, I didn't see one person buying any merchandise. Perhaps the prices were high or inventory low.

Lunch at the farm awaited us. The food was inspired by local spices that made the meal unique.

Following our feast, we had a pleasant surprise, more entertainment. This time, Uruguayan music accompanied by a singer and then two dancers performed. The show reminded me of Punta del Este ten days ago, which we all enjoyed, something positive from Francisco.

Before leaving the farm, we stopped at their small souvenir shop. I found a beautiful and unusual shaped amethyst. An addition to my stone collection.

The bus arrived back at the ship by 3:00p.m. I went straight to the ship's tour desk and asked about their Montevideo city tour and the surrounding points of interest. Surprisingly, their current tour indeed included the Jewish sites. Leah had claimed that there was a security issue. However, in the event that was true, the ship wouldn't offer the tour and take on the liability if something went wrong due to lack of security. It was another tour not adequately delivered and to be discounted, this time by Francisco's cousin. Leah's level of guiding was just as low as her cousin's. I guess it runs in the family. At least there would be no more planning by Francisco, so no more mistakes and nonsense.

After dinner and the show, I arranged a birthday celebration for Pete in the '60s lounge (my favorite era). The usual card signing, and gift giving would follow. Tonight's invitation was extended to David as well. He attended, and so a great addition to another wonderful evening.

Pete couldn't have been more appreciative. What a great guy. On every occasion, friendly and kind words from him never ceased. He always acknowledged my efforts in trying to correct Francisco's mistakes and how I continuously did my best to please everyone. Many times, Pete would commiserate with me regarding Shlomo's cruel behavior. His wife, Kiti, was the opposite.

The lovely night at the lounge continued with the oldies but goodies, songs from our teenage years. But now, being a bit older and a lot wiser, or shall I say, being a lot older and a bit wiser. We danced to the nostalgic and romantic music. Before everyone dispersed to their cabins, I reminded them that tomorrow at 10:00a.m., in the buffet, I am closing the tour accounts. See you then and there.

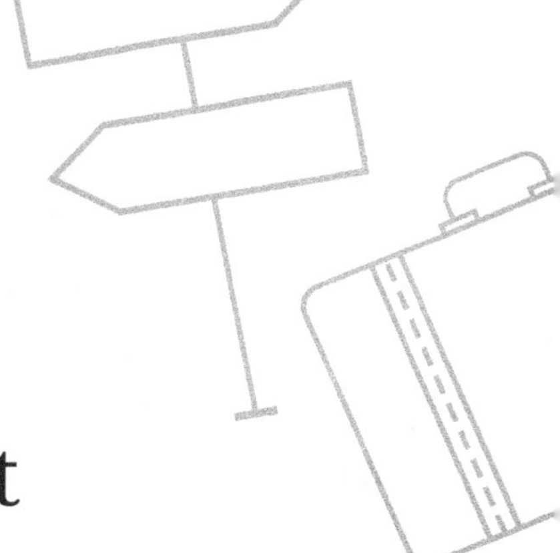

CHAPTER 33

Cruelty at Its Best

Friday, February 27

A DAY AT SEA, SOMEWHERE in the Atlantic Ocean.

At last, we'd made it to the final 24 hours of the doomed trip. No one was happier than me as we sailed back to the starting port in Buenos Aires.

This day had been designated for settling the bus tour accounts. My basic guidelines were the following:

- The only successful tour (worthy of full payment) was in Punta del Este, Uruguay.
- The chaos (not even a tour) in São Paulo, no one would pay a dime for their precious time.
- The rest of the tours were downright unprofessional, thus substantially discounted.

At 10:00a.m, as scheduled, I went to the buffet dining room and waited for the group. Since everyone arrived on time, I made a quick decision to have a short meeting.

I announced, "From the beginning of the trip, most of you complained about Francisco's mistakes and wrong leadership. At the time, I did not want anyone to dislike this unprofessional guide more than each of you already

did, as I believed it would have done further harm. So, I chose to take the blame for most of his mistakes, thinking it would be the lesser of the two evils. My intention was to expose all of his wrongdoing once we'd returned home. However, after the extremely late and dangerous transfer to the Parade's stadium, which caused us agony for hours. Now I'm asserting the truth, that practically all mistakes were Francisco's. The huge mistake that I made, was to hire him. "Some of you are repeat clients and the rest were referred to me by someone we both know and trust. My pattern of planning trips was always a success."
End of announcement.
Important Note: At this point it would have been a perfect place and time to remind the group that I warned and gave correct instructions regarding Francisco's 8:00p.m. late transfer to the Parade. Unfortunately, my blackout from Shlomo's threat aimed at the entire group not to follow my 'correct' instructions prevailed.
End of note.

I started the account closures. Once each couple or individual paid, they left the buffet area to enjoy a wide range of activities available during the last day on the high seas. Almost all the accounts were paid without incident. Why not have a problem free session? The following three couples had an issue:

1. Goldfinger: He stood directly in front of me and couldn't look straight into my eyes. The brute said, and I quote, "I don't have cash or a check with me, I'll wire you the money when I get back home." Was he kidding? All through the trip, he'd shown

off his wealth, and now he is claiming not to have money or a check with him. I didn't believe a word he said, because months before the trip, I advised the entire group in writing that bus tours would be paid in cash or a check on the last day of the cruise. All group members were aware of my terms and conditions. Now a new liar came into my life. Something was fishy above the water. Because Goldfinger is Kiti's uncle, and I knew her well, accepting his verbal promise was the only option on the table. I took into consideration that Kiti was well compensated for referring her uncle, together with two other couples, Jack and Jacqueline, Sam and Samantha (Goldfinger's friends). Having said that, good faith goes both ways and it's implied that Kiti should address any issue that may arise regarding the ones she'd referred to me and was paid for handsomely.

2. Nate and Nancy: The couple residing in the UK surprised me with a copy of their bank statement showing an exchange rate fee of $32. It was the prepaid deposit to the hotel in Buenos Aires. This character simply deducted said sum from what he owed me, because he lives in the UK I didn't have to pay for his banker's fees. How low can he go? I found it to be very rude and classless. So, what's new with some dreadful tour members…

3. Shlomo and Sharon: They were always first on every bus tour. Now, the dictator and his *lovely*

> wife were the last in line to settle their account, I wondered why? Sharon sat across from me, while Shlomo loomed beside her, he extended his famous index finger rather close to my face, if any closer I would have alerted the ship's security as David's private number was always with me.

Then the dictator opened his big mouth, it released a horrible scent, probably the onions he had for breakfast. I moved my chair backward, avoiding regurgitating from the odor. He started to shout with all his might, "Where did you buy the tickets for the Parade?" I was bewildered and dumbfounded not knowing his motive for the irrational question. The deranged man repeated his demand for an answer several times, and then went on a tirade. I was literally shaking from his animalistic behavior. The hard-hearted wife did nothing to stop the madman's verbal abuse. My pulse elevated by the second. I probably turned white and became a candidate for a nervous breakdown on this doomed trip. Only then I figure out why this couple orchestrated to be last in line, so... absolutely none of the tour members would be present to witness the dictator's intentional attack. They prevailed, no one witnessed the severity of what I just endured. Surely, my strong feeling was that Jack, the jerk, briefed Sholomo about our conversation at the buffet, two days ago. Jack for sure added on some lies, as I predicted. Not wanting to spend another heartbeat next to the mad and heartless creature, I gathered my files without settling their tour account and left the uglier-than-ugly scene.

While proceeding to my cabin with a severe headache, I also felt something alarmingly out of the ordinary with my breathing. By coincidence, the medical facility was on my way, so I paid a visit. After I briefed the doctor about the stressful experience, he examined me. My blood pressure had seen better days. However, the physician said not to worry. He gave me a remedy for my shaky situation and advised me to follow up with my medical provider back home.

I returned to my cabin for some unwinding. While doing so I came to terms with the fact that Shlomo has severe anger at life and the Creator. He desperately needed professional coaching for his troubled, juvenile behavior. This was the first time that he had traveled with me on my group trips, and he'd better believe it was the last.

Having no pep for anything, including pretending that all was well, I had to follow my instinct and make the difficult decision to cancel the group's get-together. I called my favorite officer and asked if we could meet right away.

He said, "Sure."

After one glance at me, David asked, "Conny, why are you so pale?"

I proceeded to tell him all that I'd just been through with Shlomo and then went on telling him about the others who made my life miserable.

David was totally shocked and said, "I noticed from day one that you gave the group your all."

Huh? He had only seen the tip of the iceberg regarding what I had done for the group. David's kind words were appreciated.

He further stated, "I'm so sorry for all you've gone through."

With teary eyes and heartfelt emotions, I thanked him again and gave his well-deserved gift. We wished each other the best and said our shaloms. I then made my way back to the cabin just in time to collapse on my bed from the medication that made me lethargic. Packing could wait until early the next morning. I soon fell asleep.

While sporadically waking up throughout the night, I had many thoughts running through my mind, so I made some practical decisions. Shlomo's attack will remain on the back burner for the time being. Anyhow, no one would ever believe the severity of his stormy attack. If Alex knew about the brutal meltdown, it probably would've resulted in a scene. He had enough of the madman's militant behavior. The last thing we needed on this trip was another unpleasant confrontation. So, for the time being, I would keep Shlomo's attack away from Alex.

It dawned on me, the dictator and his lovely wife owed me a thank you for their Falls tour, but, now an apology as well. Holding my breath was not an option, because manners and civility does not exist in their world. I guess mom-and-pop from both sides didn't stress good manners.

Note: The theory of having Shlomo as a pied piper had backfired. In fact, post trip, I learned that some other couples had taken interest in my trip, however, when they heard that Shlomo and Sharon were part of the group, they declined joining the South American adventure. Gee, I wonder why? End of note.

CHAPTER 34

Not a Moment Too Soon

Saturday, February 28

At the crack of dawn, we arrived in Buenos Aires, not a moment too soon. The doctor's visit did me a world of good. I'd regained my strength and was ready to take on the final day of the doomed trip and then the flight back to the States.

After breakfast, everyone disembarked the beautiful ship that accommodated us for the last 13 nights.

Alex and approximately half of the group had flights before noon. They all headed directly to the airport. The remaining tour members, including Ruth and I, were scheduled for midnight flights.

Reminder: while in the planning phase, I'd suggested that the travelers with night flights reserve a half-day accommodation at the same hotel where we'd stayed at the beginning of the trip. The owner gave me a very special low rate. Only two couples declined this arrangement: Shlomo and Sharon as well as Marty and Miriam. The foursome became good friends during the trip, and so they elected to hang around the hotel's lobby and vicinity until the evening ride to the airport.

End of reminder.

The late flyers proceed to the hotel with shared taxis for a day's stay. Upon arrival, the room keys were all ready for the downsized group.

The front desk manager said, "Mrs. Connors, I'm giving you the only suite we have. It happens to be available. Enjoy your stay."

I was so touched by his kindness and generosity.

Darling Ruth had a wide smile, but not for long.

I told her, "We're going to do a big mitzvah ("good deed" in Hebrew) by forfeiting the suite to the four room-less."

My cutie stepmom gave me a look as if she was going to kill me any minute and said, "My dear Conny, Shlomo is not worthy of your goodness and generosity. He didn't treat you nice at all. Such a person doesn't deserve another crumb from you."

She was absolutely correct, however, I replied, "I'll fight back with humanity and morality. Why not show kindness to the unkind by doing good deeds? Karma will eventually supersede. After lunch, I'll arrange another room for us, we don't need a suite."

Her face still showed disapproval. As always, she was right.

I then approached the four wanderers and told them, "Here's the key to my suite. There's plenty of room for two couples to be comfortable until the evening. Enjoy your stay."

They were so happy and pleasantly surprised, however, absolutely no words of gratitude escaped from the mouths of Shlomo or Sharon. Miriam and Marty expressed their appreciation.

The pizza was delicious, and a glass of local beer that Ruth and I shared hit the spot, but it soon made us tipsy. A long nap awaited just as soon as I arranged another room.

The nice manager said, "Mrs. Connors, why are you getting another room? Isn't the suite big enough for two petite ladies?"

After I briefed him about the two room-less couples, he told me, "I'll be right back."

No sooner than later, he returned and gladly announced, "Here's a key to room number 18" (that number is a symbol of life in the Jewish faith.) He further stated, "It's on the house."

I was thrilled and amazed at his repeated generosity.

I turned to Ruth and told her, "Remember what I said about good karma? We're not being charged for the room. Let's take a nap, my eyes are drooping."

The beer must have been very potent.

While we were on our way to the room, here came ten *lovely* people, the two formerly room-less couples, Jack and Jacqueline, Sam and Samantha, and Goldfinger with his wife. All of them were probably planning a lunch rendezvous.

I noticed that Shlomo, the dictator, spotted Hellen and Matilda as they approached the five couples.

Shlomo announced, "Let's get out of here before they follow us."

Hellen heard him and said, "We don't want to go with you anyway."

I snorted. Yeah, right! During the 20 days, she'd tried with all her might to capture Shlomo's attention, any old way she could, perhaps seeking an invitation to his fancy parties. The dictator couldn't stand the sight of Hellen, and neither did most of the group. Her mouth had no barriers, and the behavior was beyond control. Really, she's good for nothing.

The entourage of ten exited the hotel by turning right onto the sidewalk. Hellen and Matilda turned left, while Ruth and I proceeded straight to our room. Probably, within 18 seconds or less, both of us would be dreaming. After a great nap, we were relaxed and ready to face the final hours of the doomed trip.

Still having some time before transferring to the airport, both of us agreed on high tea (no more beer for Ruth and me). On our way back to the hotel, I stopped at a liquor store and bought a bottle of wine for the nice front desk manager who had gone beyond his call of duty to accommodate us.

In the evening, we shared taxis to the airport and arrived in a timely manner. Everyone proceeded to their respective airlines.

Ruth and I didn't synchronize our round-trip flights because she did not join the Falls tour. Her arrival was three days later than mine. In a major coincidence we were on the same flight and had seats right next to each other all the way back home. The first-class cabin was heavenly, as expected, for that luxury, I exhausted all my saved mileage.

During the long flight, we talked at length about the trip. Ruth's opinion regarding the social skill of some tour members were not positive by any means, and Francisco's all-around behavior displayed very poor standards. With her beautiful blue eyes, she saw fairness and practiced diplomacy.

I was thinking long and hard about my legal options. Francisco's mistakes and problems costed me a fortune and getting any reimbursement from him would likely be a steep uphill battle.

Dear Varda,
We could not have asked for a better travel agent than you!!!
Your time and deep commitment has not gone unnoticed,
You will always be highly recommended by us to others,
Thank you once again, Sarah & Hanan Greenberg.

PART 3

Post trip

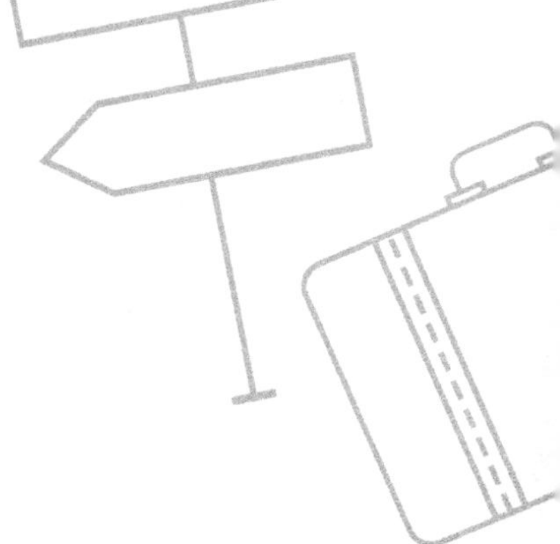

CHAPTER 35

Homecoming

Sunday, March 1

As DOROTHY SAID, "THERE'S NO place like home."

Returning to my greatest comfort zone, I felt as if a ton of bricks were lifted from my petite shoulders. Before unpacking, I prioritized sending the checks to the lucky four couples that had canceled the trip and are waiting for the refund of the Parade's tickets.

Fewer than few travel agents resell something that had already been sold, especially on international transactions outside familiar territories.

As I wrote the checks, I reflected upon what I had endured during the trip, and all with such a busy schedule filled with every imaginable circumstance, from excellent to an almost deadly situation. Where did I find the time and energy to resell eight Rio Carnival Parade tickets to people whom I didn't know? Well, it's like the saying goes, "You gotta do what you gotta do", especially while verbally committed, and I did it.

Really, the ones who'd canceled lucked out twice by:

1. Not having to weather some very tense and dangerous hours under Francisco's planning.

2. Salvaging approximately 90 percent of the money they'd spent on the Parade tickets, which is always a no-money-back event, like any other concert worldwide.

The checks were in the mail the same day I arrived home. My "mission accomplished," and that felt good. Certainly, all were happy to receive their hard-earned money.

What didn't feel good was the possibility that I'd have to face Francisco in court, if indeed, he'd reject paying me for his never-ending mistakes, handmade by the guide himself. Regardless, for the moment, nothing will be done until I'll recover my precious needlepoint.

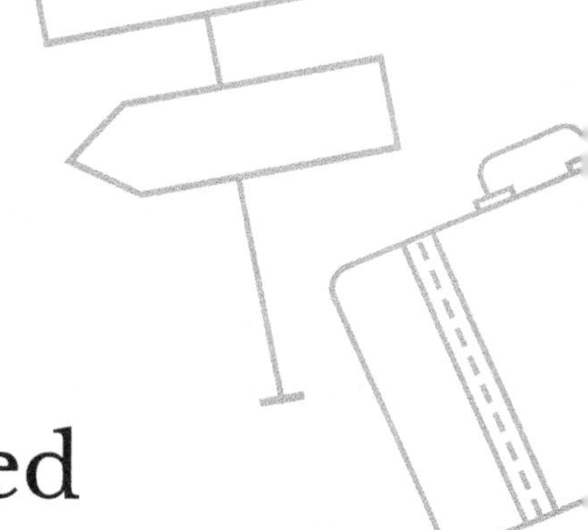

CHAPTER 36

Liabilities Granted

I RESTED AND RESTED SOME more. It took me a few days getting back on my daily routine.

I am a huge believer that a promise is a form of liability. Having said that, my next mission was dispensing the following two promises.

First, the infamous jerk from Arizona, to whom I'd promised a refund for totally missing Rio Carnival Parade, because of the unbearable and dangerous transfer.

Note: Had I not been in my memory black-out, Jack could only dream of a $900 refund from me. He and the entire group were warned about Francisco's extremely late 8:00p.m. pickup time for the Parade. I'm generous, but not stupid. This amount will be added to the debt that Francisco would owe me for covering his never-ending mistakes, throughout the trip.

End of note.

Second, the $50 tip that Shlomo gave Francisco which he demanded to be returned.

Reminder: After the Parade, while on the bus waiting for the lousy guide so we could proceed back to the ship, Shlomo had announced loud and clear, "I demand my $50 tip back from Francisco."

Determined to avoid a possible scene, I quickly calculated, as best I could, and told Shlomo that I would refund him Francisco's tip.

End of reminder.

Gladly, I wrote the two checks. In the event Francisco would not pay his debts, I'll see him in court. Therefore, my $50 refund check to Shlomo, would be an elite evidence.

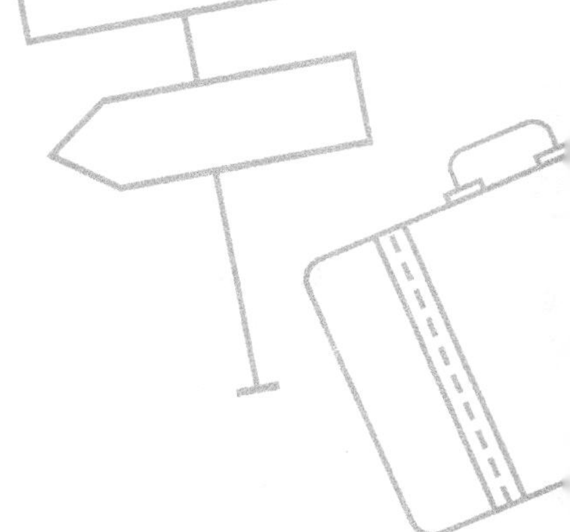

CHAPTER 37

Liabilities Owed

So far, all the people whom I'd committed refunds, were fully paid. It was a good feeling! At that point, I was free to focus on the monies owed to me, from two couples.

First: Goldfinger, the one who made sure that every tour member knew of his great wealth. He made a promise the day we settled the tour accounts by announcing and I quote, "I don't have cash or a check with me, I'll wire your money as soon as I get back home."

Ten days after the trip, nothing had been wired to my bank account, as he'd vowed. My intuition was giving me the thumbs-down. I made several phone calls, which he declined to accept. So, my intuition prevailed, and my money remained in his bank account.

Reminder: on board the ship, when I gathered the three couples, at the French restaurant, the issue was the $900 reimbursement for the missed Parade. Goldfinger said, and I quote, "I don't need your money." Well, after all that's said and done, he did need my money. What a dirty trick from a dusty Jew.

End of reminder.

With no other choice, I called his famous niece, Kiti knew of her uncle's tours being unpaid, and the promise to wire me his payment upon arriving home. I reminded her about the very generous referral fee that she was awarded from me for the three couples. That payment warrants some responsibility on her part. I asked if she'd assist me in recovering her uncle's debt, and the 'cat's meow' indicated that she didn't want to be involved. I terminated all contacts with her. There was no need for me to have another dishonest person in my world.

In my opinion, Goldfinger is worthy of being called a liar, and since his actions were a form of theft. That's another title called 'thief.'

Second: Shlomo and Sharon, their tour account was not closed on board the ship due to the madman's attack on me. I sent them an invoice, with a self-addressed stamped envelope as a courtesy.

Days later, Sharon called me seeking a resolution to a specific question, regarding their tour invoice.

After receiving a satisfactory explanation, she said, "The check will be in the mail today."

I thanked her, took a deep breath and continued with what I wanted to ask her, "Sharon, I'll get right to the point. You and your domineering husband were granted a practically two-for-one Iguazu Falls tour. To date, I have never received any form of appreciation from either one of you. How come?"

She replied, "Oh, I told you that the Falls were beautiful."

Then I replied, "Yes, indeed they were beautiful, however, stating their beauty does not constitute any form of thanks."

I paused, and still no acknowledgment of any kind. Oh well, I guess people either have manners, or they don't. Those two clearly didn't.

I further pressed, "When your anger-driven husband had a tantrum on me, the day I settled the tour accounts, why didn't you shut his oversized mouth?"

She merely said, "Oh Conny, you know him."

I exclaimed, "Oh no! Had I known him to have such extreme temperament and a pattern of cruel behavior, both of you would never have joined my group."

After a few seconds of silence, Sharon said, "Now I have a question for you, Conny."

I replied, "I'm all ears."

She then asked, "Where did you purchase the Parade tickets?"

I replied with a bit of an attitude, "Why are you asking such a strange question? Wasn't it obvious that Francisco purchased the tickets? Who else could it be? Furthermore, I had the invoice in my cabin from Francisco, itemizing Rio Carnival Parade tickets, the transfer, and parking fee for the bus. Couldn't your hardheaded husband ask me that very same question, in a civil manner, instead of attacking me? This issue could have been easily solved without your husband's barbaric outburst."

Silence fell over the conversation.

Then Sharon spilled out the bombastic statement, and I quote her, "On the cruise, Jack specifically told us, that you, Conny, wholeheartedly admitted purchasing the Parade tickets from a mafia."

Holy cow! I thought a bomb landed on me.

My attitude escalated to anger and I said, "Listen, and listen to me very carefully, please do not interrupt my explicit description of what really and truthfully happened."

I proceeded to go into full detail about Francisco's assertion that the Parade was owned/managed by a mafia. It seemed as though I was told this fact more times than I bargained for.

At the end of my intensive and comprehensive explanation, I further stated, "That was my exact answer when Jack asked me the same question on board the ship, after we returned from the ruined experience at the Parade. So, Jack, the jerk, lied to you and your raging husband."

Almost out of breath, as I was done telling Sharon the truth and nothing but the truth.

She replied, "Wow Conny, I believe your side of the story one hundred percent. It was a terrible piece of gossip from Jack. I should have addressed this awful issue with you while we were still on the trip, so the entire group could have heard that Jack lied. He was totally wrong to say that you purchased Parade tickets from the mob. Now, I know you had nothing to do with any mafia."

I thanked Sharon for the understanding and asked her to please inform any other tour members that she was in touch with, to clear up this very sensitive issue. In any case, I would not hold my breath, on account of Sharon doing so, since it's known that a lie can travel halfway around the world, while the truth is still putting on its shoes. How unfortunate, that the whole group was probably involved with the jerk's gossip and I knew nothing of his fabricated lie during the entire trip. It was a very disturbing piece of information that Jack created

What a 'zona' from Arizona. This four-letter word is an extremely vulgar term in Hebrew, and it applies to both genders. In my opinion, Jack the jerk earned another title. The sick minded jerk's karma would someday come to light…and it did.

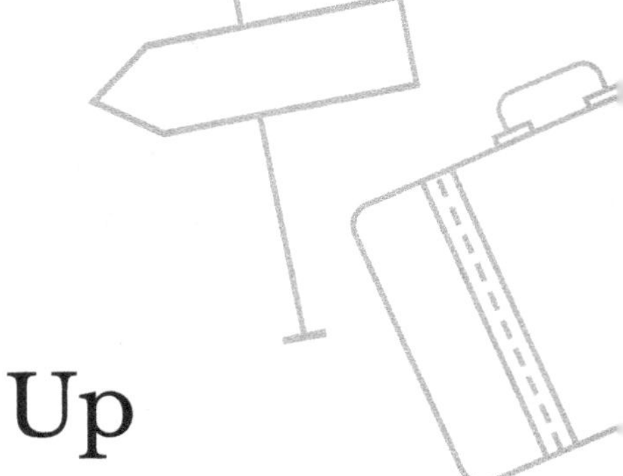

CHAPTER 38

Finally Waking Up

ALEX AND I HAD BREAKFAST at our favorite delicatessen. There was much to talk about including family, friends, the newly renovated house, old business, and an adorable new Maltese named Mish-Mish, ("apricot" in Hebrew).

Somehow, the word, **warning**, came up while I was speaking and it lit a spark in my memory. Oh my God! I suddenly recalled the distinct warning that I had given the entire group about Francisco's disastrously late 8:00p.m. pickup to the Parade! I also remembered Shlomo's index finger aimed threateningly right at the faces of all tour members, bullying them not to follow my instructions (which were definitely correct) for a proper transfer to the Parade's stadium. That atrocious scene by Shlomo had caused my nerves so much stress that it led me through a serve weeks-long blackout, and now I finally woken up. Sweat covered me from head to toe. After a quick breakfast, I immediately stopped at the bank to cancel the jerk's check. I hoped he hadn't cashed it yet, because he absolutely didn't deserve the refund. After all, he was at the emergency meeting when I gave the group correct information. Jack and Jacqueline's loyalty towards the dictator caused them (and two other couples) to totally miss Rio Carnival Parade, the theme and reason for the trip.

Reminder: At the time when I mailed Jack the jerk's check, I was still suffering from my memory blackout. Unfortunately, canceling the check was a no go as it had been cashed the day prior. Oh well, hopefully I'll be able to recover this significant amount from Francisco, if not, seeing him in court became a reality.
End of reminder.

On a more serious note, that day, I received bad news. Wonderful Pete had lost a dear family member. Alex and I planned to pay him a condolence visit in the late afternoon.

Lo and behold, but not surprisingly, Shlomo and Sharon were there to support Pete as well. At some point in the evening, I sat on the opposite end of the sofa from the dictator.

I approached him and asked, "Did your *lovely* wife inform you of our conversation?"

He only said, "Yeah."

However, no feedback or remorse came from the unmerciful big mouth.

I further asked, "Do you remember your threat to the group after I gave correct instructions regarding how and when to arrive at the Parade's stadium on time?"

I wondered what happened to the busybody's big mouth. Did it need a tune-up from being overused?

I continued, "Do you recall Jack's statement that I admitted purchasing the Parade tickets from a mafia?"

He said, "Vaguely."

I replied, "Your wife dismissed the accusations once she heard the truth from my side. Couldn't you have asked me during the trip, in a civil manner where I purchased the Parade tickets? Gladly, I would've explained the fabricated story created by Jack and even shown you the paid invoice of that purchase, thus placing the huge lie, from a jerk to rest."

Shlomo could not think of a rational answer.

I proceeded, "Do you recollect your attack on me, when I settled the tour accounts? Your brutal behavior sent me to visit the ship's medical facility."

The miserable beast said, and I quote, "None of that is relevant."

Being dumbfounded, I asked him, "Did you say not relevant?"

He nodded his head. I could no longer stand this character's audacity. It was time to disclose what actually happened, and relay the truth to all the tour members, about the cruelty that I endured with Shlomo, and some of his constituents. Within days I composed a detailed letter to the entire group, spelling out the vicious behavior from three henchmen:

- Shlomo's attack, which drove me to see a physician at the ship's medical facility
- Goldfinger's form of theft, by not paying for any of his tours
- Jack, the jerk's, fabrication, that I'd purchased the Parade tickets from a mafia

How would one even do that? Search online for the Brazilian mafia's phone number? Fabricating lies is never proper and those carrying the truth will eventually prosper.

I mailed the letters to each tour member, including the three inhumane characters. I'm sure the trio didn't favor my honest and true correspondence. However, I as well did not fancy what the evil, and uncultured creatures did to me. Retaliation was a sure expectation from the triplet ignoramuses.

CHAPTER 39

Good News for a Change

A FEW DAYS LATER, MY phone rang. The caller's ID revealed Francisco's number. My heart started to race.

Reluctantly, I picked up the receiver and heard the voice of the person who makes me gag, "Hi, Conny, I have good news for you."

There was a pause and I replied, "I'm always ready for good news."

Happily, he announced, "I have a client by the name of Rose. She's taking a trip to South America next month. One of her stops will be the Brazilian side of the Iguazu Falls. I asked her if she'd be okay bringing your needlepoint back with her to the States. The lovely lady agreed."

Francisco further told me, "I instructed Bernardo, the manager of the Falls (Brazilian side), to make sure the needlepoint would be delivered to Rose's hotel room in a timely manner."

He also informed me the date she would arrive home. I immediately jotted it down on my calendar and provided my FedEx account number, to cover the cost of the shipment.

Before terminating the conversation with Francisco, I took advantage of his call and told him all about Jack's lies and gossip, that I purchased Parade tickets from a mafia.

I further said, "Francisco, you told me many times, during our planning phase, that Rio Carnival Parade organization is owned/managed by a mafia, kindly put your statement in writing."

He answered, "Surely, I'll do that. No Problem."

Within a few heartbeats, he said, "No, actually, I will not."

It didn't come to me as a surprise that he'd changed his crooked mind so fast.

Regardless, I thanked him for attending to my needlepoint's recovery and said, "Goodbye."

Being civil to unethical lying guide was not easy to do, but for the sake of my missing precious item, I'd have to act as if I was Mother Therese with him. Challenging Francisco in any way, shape, or form would jeopardize the fate of my needlepoint. Though I was delighted that my belonging is getting closerto recovery, I had strong misgivings about this character and recovering my personal item.

He was trouble waiting to happen.

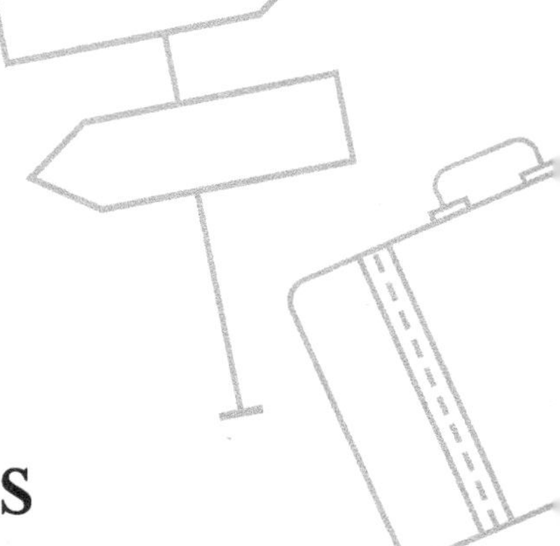

CHAPTER 40

More Complaints

THROUGHOUT THE TRIP, FRANCISCO HANDED out his business card to anyone who would take it. This was unethical to do without my permission, but Francisco's ethical pattern of conducting business had no ethics whatsoever.

Having said that, a few group members called me with complaints regarding the lying guide's misleading's.

My reply to the complainers was, "I'm sorry for what you went through, however, I already admitted, apologized, and compensated the whole group for their ruined experiences. In the event you don't have Francisco's contact, I'll provide it so you can make your own complaints to him directly."

In actuality, the biggest complainer was me, having lost thousands of dollars by greatly discounting almost every bus tour. The nasty task which awaited me was a confrontation with Francisco, regarding reimbursement for his mistakes. For sure, it would be an uphill battle, and it'll take place only after the safe return of the needlepoint. I didn't want my precious canvas to face any more consequences. Francisco is not to be trusted and taking any action against him at this time, was not an option, hopefully later on.

Days later, and rather early in the morning, the phone rang. It was Francisco. I feared he might be calling to tell me that Rose changed her mind, and she wouldn't bring the needlepoint. My heart started to race, but before long, I realized that his call was a result of some complainers who had complained directly to him.

Like a madman, he shouted, "Because of your cheap group, I'm ashamed to say that I'm Jewish, and I do not want the $235 lousy tip from any of your despicable tour members, so I am sending it all back to you. I'll also add $165 a total of $400. This amount is for goodwill only, and nothing more."

I then answered, "Please, Francisco, I appreciate the goodwill, but it's not necessary to return your tip."
Note: I knew better than to argue with the lunatic, about what I really thought of him and his never-ending mistakes, blended with lies. Doing so would cause my canvas to face a greater risk than it already had. My back was against the wall.

He continued, "If you don't cash the $400 check you'll never see your needlepoint again."

I replied, "Please email me what you just said."

He replied, "Okay, you want an agreement, I'll write one."

I started to feel overwhelmed and answered, "I did not mention anything about an agreement, however, I did ask you to please email me what you just stated, regarding your terms for the return of my needlepoint."

Francisco did his usual repeating, "If you don't cash the $400 check and sign the agreement, I'm about to write up, you'll never see your needlepoint again."

Of course, he was upset about the complainers that came his way, after all, they had the right to complain regarding his mistakes and poor guidance.

While we were still on the phone, the lying guide composed an agreement assuring him freedom from all liabilities, lies, and mistakes that he had made.

The original agreement

This is an agreement between Conny Connors and Francisco.

After all the services provided to Conny by Francisco in South America, including Buenos Aires, Iguazu Falls, Montevideo, Punta del Esti, Rio de Janeiro and São Paulo. Conny had two complaints. One of the complaints was with the tour bus in São Paulo and the second complain was with one of the transfers in Rio de Janeiro, Brazil.

Even though the full amount was paid to the bus companies and we agreed that once paid, the funds were non refundable which the proof of the non refundable condition is signed and initialed by Conny and Francisco, as proof.

Francisco is offering a refund of $400 to Conny, in a form of a check, per good customer service. Francisco is also sending Conny's needlepoint.

Francisco is demanding that Conny sign this agreement and cash the $400 check. Only then, she will recover her needlepoint.

After this agreement is signed by both parties, Francisco is mailing the needlepoint to Conny and no further claims will be done. This means no money claims from neither party.

<u>Conny signed and dated</u>
Signature Date

<u>Francisco signed and dated</u>
Signature Date

Francisco only allowed me to include two sentences in the agreement, which are in paragraph five. I'll repeat it: *"Francisco is demanding that Conny sign this agreement and cash the $400 check. Only then, she will recover her needlepoint."*

I couldn't believe that he agreed to include my input. Most probably, he did not know that his act of forcing me to cash the check, in lieu of my personal possession, is a form of extortion, and it's illegal. Clearly, he wrote it in the agreement. I left well alone. We both signed and dated the contract.

When his check of $400 arrived, I reluctantly cashed it. Whatever it would take for the safe return of my missing item, I'd oblige.

While at the bank, after signing Francisco's check, I asked the teller to print a copy, front and back, in the event that I'll take legal measures against Francisco, his cancelled check would be another vital piece of evidence to the court.

At this point and time, I made up my mind that I will face Francisco in court however, for the sake of my precious handmade project, no legal action would be pursued until the needlepoint is back in my hands. There was no other choice for me but sit patiently and wait for its arrival.

Days later, and according to my calendar, Rose should have arrived home. I waited another week and still nothing from her. I then called Francisco seeking a reason why I didn't receive my needlepoint.

The liar told me, "She lost your address."

I asked, "Why didn't you give it to her again? Please provide me with her phone number."

Nothing was said. Silence fell over the conversation. This was surely another lie from the liar. I had a strong feeling that Francisco would call Rose immediately, telling her to forward my needlepoint to his address rather than mine. Within a week, I was finally reunited with my prized possession.

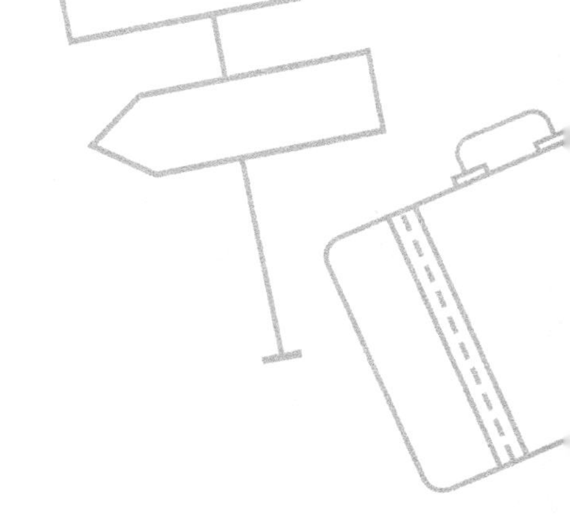

CHAPTER 41

Keeping Two Ladies Apart

My prediction was right on the money. The canvas had been sent via FedEx from the liar's address, not Rose's. Shrewd Francisco had figured out that if Rose was the one to FedEx my package, I'd have her full contact from the sender's label and I would've reached her. He was right. It's obvious that two ladies, though complete strangers, had hired the same agent to arrange their travel plans in South America. Thus, they were likely to exchange notes on their experiences. I desperately wanted to connect with Rose, but sneaky Francisco ensured that it would never happen. Rose deserved a huge thank you from the bottom of my heart, for doing such a huge favor. Imposing her with the responsibility of schlepping an item that belongs to an unknown person took chutzpah. Her good will was and still is much appreciated.

Nevertheless, I was elated and grateful for the return of my long-awaited canvas. Its journey wasn't over just yet. Before completion, one more trip for my traveling needlepoint was necessary. It went straight to the dry cleaners for a thorough deep cleaning. After all, the last hands touching my precious item, happened to be an individual whose energy and residue were not welcome under my roof.

Once the exhausted needlepoint was properly cleaned, I continued working on it. Within weeks, I completed the globe-trotting project. Next came framing and hanging the beauty on the western wall of my new living room.

Rose, if you read this book, I wholeheartedly thank you for being so kind to me, and please contact my publisher. I would love to speak with you.

CHAPTER 42

Returning the Tiny Tips

BEING EXTREMELY EAGER TO GET rid of Francisco's $400, which I was forced to cash, in order to regain my needlepoint. Those dollars were nothing but jinx in my life. I thought of a great idea. Since Shlomo had demanded and received a refund of his tip, due to the failed guiding, why not reimburse the four other couples that tipped the unfaithful guide. They were:

- Pete and Kiti: $35 (seven days of service)
- Goldfinger and wife: $50 (ten days of service)
- Sam and Samantha: $50 (ten days of service)
- Jack and Jacqueline: $50 (ten days of service)

Lousy guiding equals lousy tips.

I composed a letter to the couples above, with full explanations, regarding Francisco's revenge on my personal item. I gave them the option to be reimbursed for their tips.

Kiti, the cat, emailed me right away and stated, "Regretfully, we tipped Francisco, but a refund is not necessary."

Days later, I received the following reply from Jack. It's self-explanatory and in it he represented the Goldfingers, as well as Sam and Samantha.

Hi

I returned from Canada a few days ago.
while being there I met with the
and and we all
agreed on getting back the "Tips" that we
gave They asked me to represent
them on my letter to you to collect the
refund check

as you know, or not, we gave him $150.00
($50.- each couple). So please send me $150.00,
For all three ~~threes~~ of us, and they will
receive their part from me on my next
trip.

Thanks

After reading the weird letter, countless times, I needed some hours to digest Jack's infamous correspondence. Realistically, I was not ready to make any decisions regarding shelling out more money to the jerk. So, I took a break, to think and rethink, how to distribute Francisco's $400.

Since people at large are allowed a change of mind, I changed mine. It didn't take long, and I came to the conclusion that the $400 would be sent to my favorite charity and not to a jerk, which I didn't trust. Thus no more jinx from Francisco's contaminated money.

To the three couples that are waiting for their pathetic tip, an explanation was due. A letter will be sent to them soon. Each couple will receive and read the other two letters. In other words, all for one and one for all. Just as I received one letter from three couples.

My correspondence went as follows:

> Dear Sam and Samantha,
>
> There was absolutely no way for anyone to have known that I've been under a severe blackout. I consider both of you non-biased, I'm almost sure you realized that none of the tour members deserved a $900 refund from me, since I did my job, by correctly instructing the entire group, how and when to arrive at the Parade stadium. No one followed my correct instructions. Francisco's transfer and leading us to the main event of the trip turned out to be a disaster. Having said that, you nicely declined my generous refund as I

lifted my responsibilities. In the event that you're now seeking the $50 Francisco's tip, per Jack's letter. Please contact me directly, Jack is not a qualified collection agent.

Wishing you all the best. Conny

To Mr. and Mrs. Goldfinger,

During the last day on board the ship, while closing the bus tours accounts, you, Mr. Goldfinger said the following, "I don't have cash or a check with me, I will wire you the money for the tours immediately after arriving home." I took your word. As you very well know, all of my attempts to reach you have failed. Your intention was never to accept my calls nor pay for the tours taken, because you premediated this scheme during the trip. You lied to me, so you're a liar. You didn't pay your debt, so you are a cheater. To the best of my knowledge your action is a form of theft. A person committing theft is a thief. At your old age I'm sure you're aware of that fact, *dear* Mr. Goldfinger. Having said that, I changed my mind and your $50 went to a worthy organization and not a crook.

That's all, Conny.

To Jack and Jacqueline,

In a nutshell, the $900 refund, for Parade tickets, should have never crossed your mailbox. The reason being, I gave correct instructions on how and when to arrive at the Rio's stadium for the Parade, and you did not follow my directions.

If that wasn't enough tribulation, at the restaurant in Buenos Aires, the first Shabbat Eve, you Jack, ordered a second dinner, after finishing your first plate, nothing wrong with that, but what was very wrong, you refused to pay for your additional meal. The long and nasty scene created by you, caused us to be detained at the restaurant for an unnecessarily lengthy time. To end the ugly situation, my husband reached into his pocket, and pulled out $60 for your second dinner that you gorged down. Only then we were able to leave the restaurant and return to the hotel.

Having said that, I changed my mind, your $50 went to a worthy organization and not a completely untrustful person, like you.

That's all-Conny.

End of letters.

To date, I have never heard from any of the three couples. Could it be that I was in the right lane?

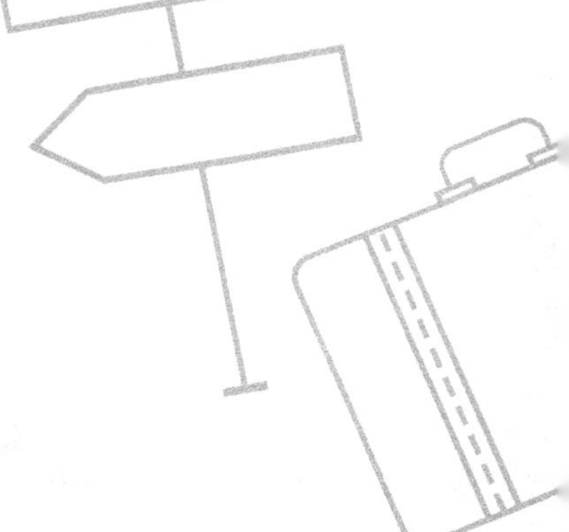

CHAPTER 43

Attorneys in Play

BEFORE SPENDING HARD-EARNED DOLLARS ON a lawyer, I thought it would be smart to begin communications with the New Jersey Attorney General. I wrote a detailed letter, laying out the lying guide's misdeeds. I soon received a response. It basically stated:

> "The only action, within the attorney general's power, is to file your complaint in our official database. If our office receives a significant number of complaints, we may then decide to open an investigation.
>
> To further pursue this issue, you could open a case with small claims court on your own or hire a lawyer."

Once receiving a response from the attorney general, I needed to clarify an issue, so I placed a call. Before terminating the conversation, the very nice clerk went out of her way to let me know that Francisco had another complaint against him, she asked me if I would like to read it.

I happily replied, "Yes, yes, yes! Please, right away!"

The clerk mailed me a copy of the complaint. Upon receipt, I opened it immediately and soaked in every word.

To: Attorney General's Office
Attn: Division of Consumer Affairs.

Re: Complaint against

In July we contacted to book a family trip for the New Year in Punta del Este. He had claimed to be a native Uruguayan who specializes in bookings there. On August 1st we had given him an initial deposit of $2500 for the accommodation in the 3-bedroom apt/condo complex. was very persuasive about the renting this place versus a hotel being " best location, most comfortable and beautiful accommodation for the family of 4". More so on August the 12th he contacted us to say he is going to "upgrade" us to a slightly smaller but better penthouse unit with great views.
We arrived Punta with vouchers in hand filled with excitement to start our vacation. To our dismay the building had no numbers or name or the street signs anywhere. was not there to meet us and the location was in the working class neighborhood, lacking any tourist comforts nearby. Finally, we found it, with help of a total stranger (no one speaks English there) and after much difficulty received the keys. We entered a small neglected apartment with holes in the walls, mold and mildew dead plants and peeling wallpaper. The place was sparsely furnished with stained bedding. It looked like the whole set up was done to trap the unsuspecting tourists!!!
Our numerous phone calls and e-mails that night were completely ignored by ..
Only the next morning after several conversations with his family members showed up.
During our tense encounter he revealed to us that he is an exclusive agent to this apartment complex
Which explains why he insisted on this booking and is not a legitimate, unbiased travel agent as he claims to be with a genuine expertise on Uruguay. Clearly, our family got ripped of for the total of $4622.40 to stay for 6 nights at a place that resembles a cheap motel.
has refused to help us to find anything else, therefore we moved out immediately, finding different accommodations in the full service hotel.
completely misrepresented and lied to us by claiming an impossibility to book something on our own for the "busy season" and charging the top prices for the inferior place. We are seeking a full refund as well as a reprimand to stop from dishonest practice to trap others!!!

Sincerely,

PS. Copy of the bill enclosed.

After reading the letter, which included the phone number of the complainant, I called and spoke to the gentleman whose family became prey of Francisco's crooked planning. We had a field day comparing notes and discovering lots of common ground, regarding our experiences with the one and only.
Reminder: Before hiring Francisco, I checked his background. No complaints had shown up yet, because the family of four that traveled to Punta del Este, Uruguay, started their vacation a month after my trip. Therefore, nothing was documented on him or his agency. End of reminder.

I suppose once Francisco received a copy of my correspondence with the New Jersey attorney general against him, he hired a cockamamie lawyer, who promptly sent me a letter suggesting that I'm defaming his client. Said letter had no phone number, street address, email, or website, only a P.O. box, city, and state.

So, I sent this odd lawyer a copy of the complaint letter from the nice family of four. I never received a reply from the strange lawyer.

Since my decision to face Francisco in court was solid, my intuition whispered, "You go girl". I started to search for vital information regarding New Jersey's Small Claims Court. I learned the following:

1. I would have to open the case in the defendant's jurisdiction. That means travelling over 2,000 miles.
2. The maximum possible award for a case, is $6,000. My losses were in that bracket

3. The court gives litigants the choice of having an attorney represent them or representing themselves.
4. There would be no recording of the court proceedings.
5. No appeal.

Too bad for me if I lose.

To minimize the risk of losing, I thought it would be wise to hire a lawyer. Who else can deal with liars? Busy as a bee, I was in search of legal representation.

Slowly but surely, I developed a list of some potential lawyers. Patiently, I started dialing one by one. To my dismay, the options slowly dwindled. No one took interest in my case. I venture to say that it was too small for their practice. Continuing my search, I came across a young female attorney named Paula.

After telling her my pathetic story, she said, "I can assist by searching previous cases similar to yours. It will help towards victory, but no promises, and I cannot represent you in court because I have a baby on the way."

I took her advice, and she soon prepared five files, which would hopefully support my case against Francisco. Paula was so fair with her fees, and had professional conduct. Too bad she couldn't represent me. Before we parted ways, I wished her well, with the expansion of her family.

Meanwhile, the last lawyer on the list did not reject me. After briefing him on my issues with Francisco, he sounded amazed and agreed to take the case. His hourly rate wouldn't break the bank, and my choices were none. I hired him. His name was Don.

My lawyer sent me his contract to read, sign, and include a check to open the case. I followed his request. There was a clause stating, "No communication shall take place with the defendant and his team, whatsoever aside from exchanging documents. That made me feel very comfortable. Little did I know that this is a standard phrase in any attorney-client contract. At that time, had I been told by a fortune teller not to hire Don, I could have saved lots of money, energy, time, and Don would have saved much more, trust me.

Immediately, I reached out to the following people:

- Maritza, the incredible local guide in Sao Paulo
- The female lawyer from Israel, she and her friend had purchased two of my eight Rio Carnival Parade tickets
- The civil/decent tour members

I asked all of the above to provide testimony in writing regarding Francisco's leadership as a guide. I specifically stated that they'd be objective. Everyone adhered in a fair manner, and my file of evidence continued to increase. I forwarded all of the documents to Don's office. Once he received the package, I supposed that he'd scrolled through it, because he called me with the following comments:

"It wasn't an easy trip with such a low functioning guide. Your evidence is concrete and totally understood. The five precedent cases that Paula prepared are a great asset. She did an amazing job, and money well spent."

I took it as a compliment.

In the course of the following days, Don and I had numerous phone conversations covering Francisco's harmful leadership.

Over the next day or so, the lying guide was served with court papers, instructing him to appear in seven weeks for the trial.

After having many sleepless nights, wondering what's waiting for me at court, as only phone conversations didn't seem to be enough. I came up with a great idea. Why not fly to New Jersey and have a thorough review with my attorney on the misguided portions of the trip that Francisco was involved in, also a good reason to meet Don in person before the trial. My mind was made up. East coast, here I come.

In the morning, I called Don regarding my plans, he didn't react favorably, furthermore, he said, "Conny, no need to fly over 2,000 miles, I have everything under control."

I asked Don what dates were open on his calendar. He checked and gave me some options.

Accordingly, I arranged a short rendezvous to sit with my lawyer face-to-face. As a world traveler, it would be a hop, skip, and jump. I predicted that between an eight-hour flight each way (door-to-door) and approximately a six-hour session with Don, this journey should take no more than 24 hours. The get-together with Don would be a worthy investment to better lay out my case. So, I thought.

A day before the red-eye flight to the east, I was thinking that it would be nice to bring my signature Middle Eastern dish for Don and his staff, a treat for lunch. After all, I was flying with no baggage, and the approaching winter weather would not spoil the food.

The same day, I received a call from Don.

He said, "Conny, since you're arriving in the early morning hours and the airport is not far from my office, I'll meet you at curbside, by the car rentals." He then gave me his license plate number.

It sounded easy and accommodating. He would provide transportation to and from his office, and I'd supply lunch. I love feeding people.

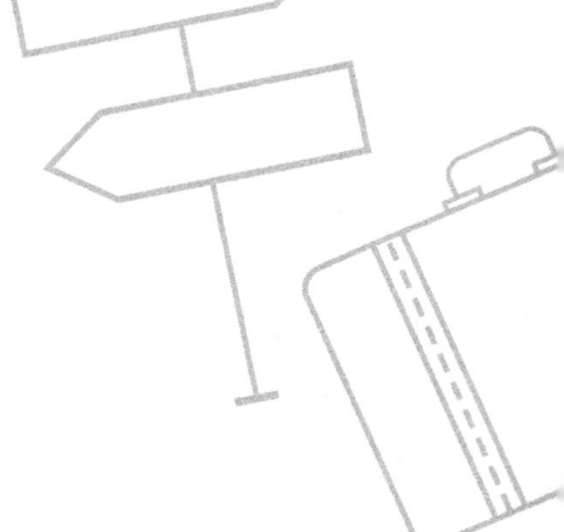

CHAPTER 44

Busy 23 Hours

During the night flight, I couldn't close my eyes. It all seemed surreal, not knowing what I'll face.

Oh well, I asked for it. Life wasn't boring during the doomed trip nor after.

The plane landed on time. My signature dish still looked fresh, thanks to the kind flight attendant who allowed me to store it in the refrigerator.

I found the designated location where Don had instructed me to wait. How strange it was standing on a curbside waiting for a male stranger.

No more than a few minutes, a car with the license plate belonging to my attorney appeared.

I waved, he stopped, and I entered the car. There was a bit of awkwardness. Had this been a blind date it would have been the last.

Oh, my goodness! The car was so cluttered with every imaginable junky item, even the color of its carpet could not be determined. I would think that a junk collector or hoarder with a law degree should have the sense to clean his car or rent a vehicle before picking up a client. I suppose he didn't know that such an expense is a tax deductible for his business.

By the time we arrived at his office, it was approximately 8:30a.m. I started to feel a little drowsy from traveling and a sleepless night. I asked Don if it was possible that I rest for a while. Gladly, he showed me a vacant room which had a reclining chair. Just what I needed, a short time to close my eyes. When I am exhausted, snoozing anywhere is no problem. Yes, I'm Jewish but not a princess.

A cup of coffee and a sandwich from home hit the spot. The office displayed cleaner surroundings than the hair-raising car and the décor looked like no changes had been made since the turn of the century.

I was ready to view the case and all of the proof that had been sent weeks ago, they were as follows:

First: The detailed letter from Maritza, the guide at Santos/São Paulo. She testified about the impossible tour that went terribly wrong and, as a result, it escalated to a dangerous situation.

Second: Two conflicting itineraries for the above cities, one from Jose given to Maritza, the other, given to me from Francisco. Both did not match.

Third: Maritza's business card, where she'd written, "Conflicting contracts! Impossible to do in one day!" She signed and dated it.

Fourth: The letter from the Israeli lawyer. She explained in full detail about the very dangerous transfer and a ruined Parade viewing.

Fifth: My canceled check of $50. Shlomo's tip given to Francisco, then demanding it's return.

Sixth: The joint letter from three couples. They requested their tip money back from Francisco.

Seventh: The agreement between Francisco and I, (It bore the two sentences suggesting extortion regarding my needlepoint) and I'll quote, "Francisco is demanding that Conny sign this agreement and cash the $400 check. Only then, she will recover her needlepoint." (Without those two sentences, I would have never opened a lawsuit.) This agreement was my key piece of proof.

Eighth: A copy of the $400 check. I believe this is important evidence, suggesting extortion.

Ninth: A copy of the complaint letter, from the family of four. They'd written to the New Jersey Attorney General, complaining how they suffered from Francisco's services, during their vacation in Uruguay.

Tenth: The packet of five precedents. It had been prepared by Paula, the pregnant attorney. Don's opinion was, "Money well spent."

Eleventh: Letters from the civil group members. These letters were complimentary of my services throughout the trip. It's hearsay, but it couldn't hurt.

In less than three hours, we were half done with my full explanation of the case. By then, lunch break was in order. Everyone in the office enjoyed the dish that traveled over 2,000 miles to reach their stomachs.

During the day, I noticed that Don did not have the friendliest staff (especially his paralegal/secretary Collette).

By 4:30p.m., we wrapped up our meeting. I felt comfortable reviewing my case in person, more so than phone conversations. I was ready for the drive to the airport, however, preferring to take a taxi. I arrived back at my doorstep, some 23 hours from when I left home for the Jersey venture.

CHAPTER 45

He's Got to Be Kidding

It took me a whole day getting over the 23-hour jaunt to and from the East Coast. My gut feeling could not provide me any clue whether I'd be on a smooth ride or a bumpy road with Don representing me, even though we met eye to eye.

To make matters further uncertain, days later, I received a call from my attorney, he said "Conny, I don't have enough evidence to support your case."

Astonished, I replied, "That's all I have, and it carries substantial weight towards victory. You even complimented me on the concrete evidence."

He continued, "Send me credentials and any document of recommendations from places you previously were employed."

Don has got to be kidding with this utterly ridiculous request. I planned to prepare his sick desire later during the week.

I then asked him, "Did you receive any documents from the defendant?"

He replied, "Everything is under control. Please, Conny, do not worry. Oh, by the way the court awarded you an entire day's session. It was taken into consideration that you will need to fly in from out of state for the upcoming trial."

Before we wrapped the conversation, Don repeated, "Don't forget to send me your credentials and all other materials from your previous employment." I shook my head in disbelief.

Anticipation grew from sunrise to sunset, and the court date was slowly approaching.

Meanwhile, I received a wedding invitation from Israel. Vivi, my childhood friend, was planning a wedding for her daughter. Noticing that the happy event would take place two days after the trial, I really wanted to reply, "Yes, I'm coming," but, I needed to think for a minute. Geographically, New Jersey is approximately one-third closer to Israel than my home state. So, if I could find a flight the morning after court, I'd arrive a day before the wedding. I'm a world traveler, so a jam-packed schedule is my familiar territory. It would be exciting to attend my friend's simhah ("happy occasion" in Hebrew).

I booked a flight (departing Newark) to Tel Aviv, so I'd be heading farther eastward. Since I'm flying to attend the wedding, I'd also visit my family and other friends for a week's stay. This should certainly be a positive change from the negative hours I will spend with Francisco all day in court, under one roof.

I then called Don advising him of the updated travel schedule and to make arrangements about sending the entire file to my home. He agreed that schlepping all the court files as well as Francisco's, halfway around the world is impractical and he committed to FedEx my package right after the trail. I thanked him and provided payment for the shipment.

My altered plan that allowed me to depart New Jersey without my files, was music to Don's waxy ears, and he couldn't be happier. I kid you not.

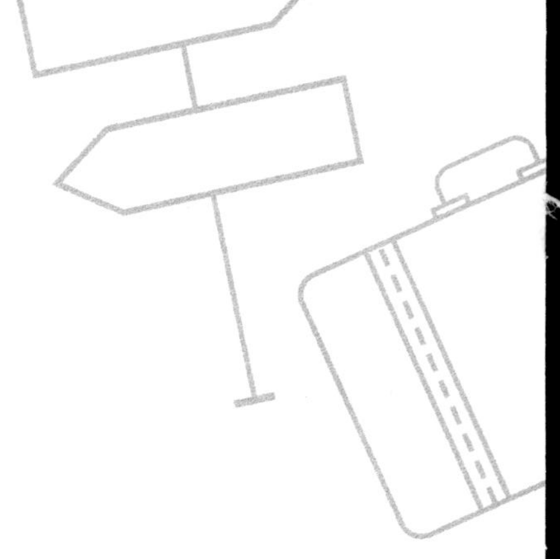

CHAPTER 46

Retaliation

Meanwhile, what's happening at the ranch with Shlomo and Sharon?

Via the grapevine and into my ears, I heard that the dictator was extremely mad for exposing the truth about his brutal behavior towards me. Well, being mad is what a madman will do. The hardships that I had endured from Shlomo, and some of his constituents throughout and post doomed trip were needless to say disturbing and worthy of exposure, such behavior is inhumane.

With that said, would anyone believe that Shlomo's retaliation was in the act of becoming buddy-buddy with Francisco? So, the dictator and wife hosted a barbecue for the lying guide—yes, the one and only Francisco. How low can one go?

Note: I never wished to know which tour members attended the fiesta. I venture to say that only the ones who tipped Francisco would have the guts to face the manipulating guide at the barbecue.

End of note.

Solely, the couple who tipped him, and very shabby, were Kiti and Pete, $2.50 per person per day. I wondered if she (the cat) remembered meowing, "I regretted tipping Francisco."

Did the backstabbing Shlomo forget the following:

- On the first day of the trip, thousands of feet in the air while flying to the Iguazu Falls, Shlomo asked me loud and clear, "Conny, did you know that the guide you hired is a liar?" I remember thinking, welcome to my world.
- During the trip, Shlomo often complained about Francisco's unprofessional services.
- On the last day, just before the dangerous transfer to the Parade, Shlomo tipped him an offensive amount, $2.50 per person per day.
- After the Parade, while we were waiting on the bus for the ride to the ship, Shlomo loudly announced, "I demand my $50 tip back!" (Which he received from me weeks later).
- The last moments with the lousy guide, Francisco said, "Goodbye Shlomo." The dictator, with his wife, ignored him and stormed off the bus to the ship.

Did Francisco, the liar, forget the following?

- He'd taken me aside multiple times during the trip to complain and make negative remarks about some tour members, especially Shlomo.
- He'd called the group at large "cheap and despicable."
- The most serious offense, Francisco had clearly stated, "I am ashamed to say I am Jewish, because of your cheap group."

If this new friendship between Francisco and Shlomo was not ass-kissing to the highest degree, I don't know what is. I cannot think of another adjective, decent or otherwise, to describe their sick relationship.

Though they hated each other, their personalities were a like. The duo shared common grounds in their characters, both are hypocrites and imposters.

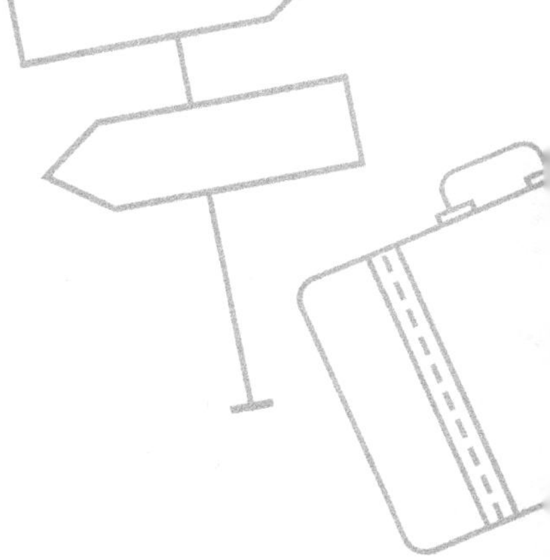

CHAPTER 47

Appreciated, but Not Needed

My second rendezvous to New Jersey was a few days away. Anticipation got the better of me.

Choosing a red-eye flight on the first trip had worked for my convenience, so I arranged the same schedule. I also booked a two-night stay at a hotel that had shuttle service to and from the airport.

This arrangement would allow me an extra day prior to the trial. Arriving in a rush would cause stress, and that wasn't necessary mainly because seeing Francisco would be stressful enough.

I was pretty much ready, willing, and able to endure a day filled with apprehension, anxiety, and shaky nerves, knowing that lies would be flying through the courtroom's roof. The fact that my lawyer had 'everything under control' eased my mind, and I was looking forward to spend a week in Israel with family and friends.

A few days before my departure to Jersey, Don called me and said the following:

"Regarding your balance due, the full session in court and some prep hours the day prior to the trial are extra.

Those charges will be in the final balance. Please sign the letter that I am about to fax to you, and return it to me."

As always, I adhered to Don's instructions.

He further said, "Since you'll arrive at the hotel in the early morning hours, I suggest you arrange for an early check-in. If possible, you should try to sneak a nap."

Did Don forget that I'm a veteran travel agent? I know what to do and say.

He continued, "My wife Michelle, will meet you in the hotel lobby at approximately 2:00p.m. She'll bring you to my office for the purpose of wrapping up any last-minute briefings of your case. At dinnertime, the three of us will go to a restaurant. Thereafter, we'll drive you back to the hotel. The following day in court will be a busy one, so be sure to get enough rest."

It was a lot of information to digest, I stored and accepted it.

The big day soon arrived, before leaving my house for the airport, I called the hotel's front desk and spoke to the night shift manager regarding my reservation. He promised to accommodate me if a room would be available upon my early arrival.

En route to New Jersey.

Around 6:30a.m., the flight landed and the airport shuttle soon took me to the hotel.

At check-in, the receptionist named Veronica gave me a friendly smile and the key to my room. A phone call to the front desk the night before greatly helped.

By 7:30a.m., a hot shower and diving into bed were the perfect combination after the red-eye flight, which turned out to be another sleepless night on the friendly skies.

At 1:00p.m., I woke up. A sandwich from home and an apple gave me enough energy for the day ahead.

Following Don's instructions, I headed to the lobby. It didn't take long until Michelle and I met.

For the life of me, I couldn't understand why the wife of my lawyer gave me a large package and said, "It's a gift for you." I thanked her and handed it to the concierge, until my return from dinner.

As I approached Michelle's car, of course, my thoughts shifted back to her husband's vehicle, remembering the clutter and then some. That memory would not vanish from my mind. Her car's condition was within the norm.

Soon, we arrived at Don's office. Before starting to review the case, I asked Don again about any feedback from the defendant.

He said, "Conny, it's all under control, do not worry."

Colette, the paralegal/secretary at the office, had an attitude towards me right off the bat. To say the least, it was very confusing. I never said one word out of line or encountered any negative issues with her. This behavior was not professional. Oh well, she has to punch a time clock, not me.

Don and I had a two-hour session reviewing the case. In the early evening, the three of us went to a restaurant in Michelle's car. At dinner, I only ordered soup and salad, not being hungry because my gut felt ominous about the next day and what was waiting for me.

After the meal, Don and his wife took me back to the hotel. On the way to my room, I passed the front desk and took the gift Michelle gave me. Whatever it contained, was appreciated, but not needed. I had no room in my suitcase to carry excess weight halfway around the globe. I was too tired to open the package. It could wait until the next day.

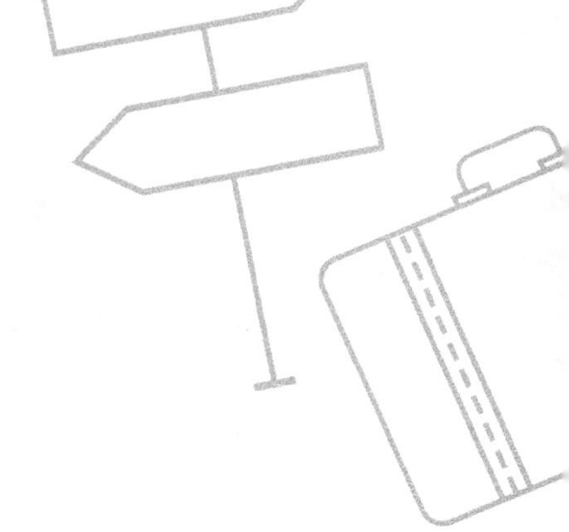

CHAPTER 48

The Trial

THE NEXT MORNING, I WOKE up before the alarm rang, was I nervous? Yes, very.

The gift from Michelle was staring at me, okay, I'll open it. Oh no, flying with three heavy glass bowls for thousands of miles, was an unnecessary weight in my small luggage. They were useful items for any kitchen, but schlepping them all the way to Israel and back to my kitchen was not practical. Knowing me, I'll somehow make it useful.

Before going down for breakfast, I wrote a thank-you note to the helpful clerk, Veronica, from the front desk. The kindness she had shown me for the early morning check-in, the day before, did not go unnoticed. I also included a tip and the glass bowls (surely, she would not have to carry them thousands of miles to her kitchen). It felt good to repay her hospitality, and I'm sure she would be delighted about the gesture.

At the restaurant, I continued to feel anxious about any potential surprises that may arise. Facing Francisco and hearing his lies was a given. No wonder I felt on edge. In spite of all that, I tried to focus on the positive side and have faith in my lawyer. This gave me a stronger sense of security, thus, my stress started to decrease. Luckily, the vegetarian omelet and all the good stuff that came with it agreed with my whirling stomach.

I had an hour before meeting Don. It was enough time to get ready for the unknown. I continued to wish and hope that it will be an easy day.

As I entered my room after breakfast, I exclaimed, "Oh my God, where's my purse?"

It was with me at the restaurant and now nowhere in sight. My passport, airline ticket, a few fine pieces of jewelry, some cash for incidentals, and the envelope containing the wedding gift were all inside my purse. I thought I'd die.

Within seconds, I was out the door. Not wanting to wait for the elevator, I flew down the stairs from the fourth floor to the restaurant (when in a hurry, I can fly). All I needed before the trial was losing my identity and other important possessions, due to my own negligence. If that wasn't enough, in a different state far away from home.

Luckily, the handbag was intact and untouched, where I left it. What a relief! As if being a basket case since arriving in New Jersey was not stressful enough. Usually, I'm very careful with my belongings, but stress can be harmful. From then on, the handbag almost became part of my anatomy. I held on to it for dear life remembering the fiasco involving my needlepoint. This lesson would not go in vain.

Returning to the room with the purse in my hand and a racing pulse, I thought, this scary sprint was not on the schedule. Trying to regain my composure and not be late for the drive to court with Don, I forfeited the time to apply makeup. My cascading, wavy hair would have to suffice. It was more important to do some deep breathing and take a short walk, inhaling fresh air. A beauty contest was not on the agenda, however, ugly interactions were not to be ruled out.

My attorney arrived at 8:30a.m. sharp. The second bombshell in one morning, soon unveiled. Surprise! The rude paralegal, Colette, was sitting up front next to Don, he approached me with a morning greeting, which I reciprocated. Of course, the thing that came along with him kept its mouth shut, by not saying anything. No skin off my back, she needs a job not me.

Truly, I always preferred not sitting in the front (with the exception of riding with my husband). Regardless, I was surprised at the lack of professionalism pertaining to this particular seating arrangement.

The clutter in the back seat looked like it had been shifted aside, making room for me to sit.

We arrived early to the courthouse parking lot. There was a fee, so Don drove around until he found a spot, on a small dark street. Before exiting the car, my thrifty lawyer told me to leave my cell phone in the glove compartment. I was assured he'd lock the vehicle, and the phone would be safe. I had to chuckle. Who in their right mind would break into such a gross-looking interior? The exterior was just as bad.

The three of us entered the court building and went towards our designated room. It was still locked, so the early birds sat in the long hallway, waiting for the doors to open. No one else had yet arrived. I felt a little special because my case was the only one on the calendar.

A quick reminder: the court had given me the whole day due to my lengthy travel schedule.
End of reminder.

For some reason, I noticed Colette wasn't in sight. I didn't ask and couldn't care less if the Jersey wind blew her all the way to Kansas.

Meanwhile, my lawyer told me, "I'm going to coach you, regarding today's session."

I replied, "I'm all ears."

He said, "You're the first to take the witness stand. I'll start asking you the questions, it's called direct examination. You are only to answer yes or no, nothing else."

I answered, "Don, I have a true story to tell with an abundance of proof that will greatly help substantiate my case."

He replied, "You are only to answer yes or no. After I'm through with my questions, Francisco's lawyer will do the asking, and that's called cross examination. I want you to look at my facial expressions at all times and accordingly you will know to stop talking immediately."

I thought, no wonder Colette took off, she probably didn't want any part of witnessing the unconventional orders from her boss, nor any reactions to the overwhelmingly dumb instructions.

Again, I thought, he's got to be kidding. How weird and unprofessional. No wonder he had me leave my cell phone in his car, so I'd have no access to call anyone about the stranger-than-strange demand.

I was unbelievably stunned, regarding the outrageous coaching. I planned to deal with it, once I'd be on the witness stand.

He continued, "When your cross examination is over, we will recess for lunch. After the noon break, Francisco will have a turn on the witness stand, for his direct and cross examinations.

Conny, the following is very important, Colette will sit between you and me, in the event Francisco is lying, whisper it to her, and she'll relay that information to me. Thereafter, I'll do the cross examination. Finally, should time allow, we will rebut until closing."

I was very uncomfortable with Don's seminar. What a joker, telling me, "If Francisco is lying." The crooked guide couldn't tell the truth, even if his tongue was notarized as being innocent/truthful. This session was totally, extraordinarily insane.

Meanwhile, we were still the only ones waiting in the long hallway. A few minutes went by and I spotted two people at the far end of the hall. At first, I couldn't identify either of them. One was a man wearing a suit, and the other, nondescript. Since I never saw Francisco in business attire, it took me several seconds to recognize him. My heart pumped faster than during the race from the hotel room to the restaurant, in search of my purse.

For sure, Francisco was coached to wear a suit, making him appear as a decent citizen. Only I knew that underneath it was a person completely devoid of character.

Don then asked me, "Do you know **that lady**?"

I said, "I don't see any lady?"

He replied, "The person that's sitting next to Francisco."

I answered, "I have no idea who that person is."

It took me a few minutes to figure out and realize who **that lady** was, ... Of course, she's Francisco's rich female friend, who is so generous to him and he bragged about her throughout the trip's planning. For sure, Don already knew **that lady's** generosity towards Francisco very well. When Don asked me earlier if I knew her, he was only testing me and was happy with my answer, that I didn't know who she was. My reply was assurance to my crooked lawyer.

The trial room opened and we were invited inside. The ones that entered from the plaintiff's team were my lawyer Don, his paralegal Collette, and Conny (yours truly). From the defendant's team Francisco and **that lady**.

The clerk Clarence had a nametag and I made a mental note. The missing were Francisco's attorney and the magistrate.

We waited for the defense attorney longer than anticipated. I supposed the magistrate would enter when all parties were in the courtroom. After the better part of 30 minutes, here came the missing defense lawyer, followed by the magistrate. Meanwhile, the clerk documented all arrivals.

Francisco's attorney was totally disoriented and confused to say the least, while huffing and puffing, he apologized to the court for being late and announced, "My mama went to the hospital this morning." This unprofessional statement seemed ridiculous and untrue, it didn't justify wasting so much of the court's time.

Almost 10:00a.m. and nothing was in progress, however the defense lawyer started fiddling with his paperwork, then the unthinkable took place before my eyes. Don walked over to the defendant's side and helped Francisco's lawyer to organize his files. He later called it "helping with house cleaning" (If anything needed to be 'cleaned,' it was Don's filthy car and not the files of the opposition). I found this to be very strange. Even stranger, the judge that looked tired witnessed this nonsense and said nothing. More unprofessional behavior from all directions.

Finally, I was sworn in to take the witness stand. Don started his line of questioning. Truthfully, none were relevant to the core of the trip's problems. He asked me about destinations and the nature of some tours. The yes and no answers did not relate to any of Francisco's failures and consequences. Worse still, he didn't present any of my evidence to the court.

Not wanting to be reprimanded by the drowsy magistrate, I was extremely fearful to ask his honor if and when I'd be allowed to display my true story and not answer yes or no only to my lawyer's question which he coached me this morning, outside the courtroom.

I elected not to ask the magistrate, because by doing so, Don could further sabotage my case. At this time, I was very nervous and bewildered. What an awful situation to be in the courtroom. Did I fly more than 2,000 miles and pay for an awful representation from my awful lawyer? I think so. The only option was hoping, wishing, and praying that the nitty-gritty of my case would come in shortly. Still no proof was presented to the court. Tough luck, nothing changed.

Within a few minutes, Don said, "I have no further questions."

I couldn't have been more shocked and disappointed.

Facing Francisco's attorney for my cross examination came next. His opening statement was extremely long and he talked an abundance of nonsense. Without exaggeration, Francisco's lawyer stood like a stiff stick and took a few minutes to review each question before asking me. It surely seemed that he was accessing court documents for the first time, a perfect excuse to stall more precious hours.

To my pleasant surprise, the tired magistrate admonished the defendant's attorney and said, "Counsel, you are taking too much time with your questions. Get to the point."

I was disappointed that the defense attorney disregarded the warning and continued with his lingering performance. The weak and tired magistrate never again reminded the slow attorney of his weird pattern, which was very obvious.

Wow, thus far, the trial was at best unprofessional and at worst, orchestrated to fail me.

For instance, after responding to an irrelevant question from Francisco's lawyer, I paused, faced the magistrate, and asked, "Your Honor, I forgot one thing. May I say it?"

Immediately, Don jumped out of his seat with a twisted rage on his face and shouted, "No, you may not!"

The exhausted magistrate said nothing to my lawyer. At that moment, I happened to make eye contact with Clarence, the court clerk. We were in shock and disbelief at what happened. I couldn't get over how the weary magistrate just sat like a statue and did not react to the pathetic action from my lawyer. Perhaps he had a sleepless night, causing him to be lethargic and inattentive. Furthermore, the judge should have been alert enough to reprimand Don by saying, "Counsel, the question from Mrs. Connors was directed to me at the bench, not you. This is my courtroom and no one over-rules me."

But the tired chief was probably yawning and missed Don's outburst.

Note: This dramatic scene would not be forgotten or go in vain. I planned to address the issue with the court upon returning home, with hopes I'd have the opportunity to get in touch with Clarence, the clerk. There wasn't much of a chance that he'd help me but trying does not hurt.
End of Note.

Within minutes the defense lawyer said, "No further questions."

In a nutshell, both my examinations couldn't have been worse, how so?:

1. My direct examination from Don was, mostly yes and no answers. Nothing else allowed.
2. My cross examination from Francisco's lawyer was nothing but non-relevant occurrences during the trip.

The trial went on recess for lunch. I couldn't look at Don, the person I trusted to represent me in court. So alone I proceeded to the cafeteria.

Don caught up to me and said, "Don't worry Conny, we'll get him when it's Francisco's turn on the witness stand."

I didn't believe a syllable from the lying attorney's mouth.

Coincidentally, after lunch we all returned to the courtroom rather early, only to find it locked.

While waiting in the hallway, Don parked his rear end next to me. I moved away from him and he said, "Conny, I forgot to tell you a couple of issues.

First: Francisco is countersuing you for his airfare to South America in the amount of $1,980."

I replied in disbelief, "Oh my God, now you're telling me? What's next?"

The liar, I mean my lawyer, further announced.

"Second: I've been informed by a reliable source that you Conny, had 'the hots' for Francisco."

This was the icing on top of any given cake! My attorney couldn't have been more unprofessional and had chosen the worst time to deliver the creepy and disgusting news. My immediate reaction was—do I cry, laugh, or run to the ladies' room and vomit my lunch?

This most nauseating news made me think that dying on the spot would not be such a bad idea. I was beyond mortified, being that:

- I'm old enough to be Francisco (young) mother
- I am not into men who are into other men
- I'm in a monogamous marriage with the most wonderful man
- I couldn't stand Francisco from his first lie

Unfortunately, it surfaced after he received most of the non-refundable money.

Such extreme gossip definitely came from jealous minds and filthy mouths, aka some tour members. My blood ran cold, together with a burning mind. Attempting to process a meritless accusation was not on the agenda.

Feelings of loathing for Don and Francisco grew by the minute.

A few thoughts reached my bewildered mind:

1. The series of compliments that Francisco had bestowed upon me at the Falls tour—had the gossipers/vibers twisted Francisco's compliments into a nasty rumor? Thank God I didn't go to the casino with him during the Iguazu Falls tour.
2. It seemed to me that some tour members such as the dictator, the jerk, or even Hell-en were in touch with my dishonest lawyer.
3. How and who else would deliver this despicable information? Trashy mouths create more garbage.

Within seconds of Don delivering this catastrophic news, the doors opened and we entered the trial room for Francisco's turn on the witness stand. Truly, I was sick to my stomach and overwhelmed at the sight of him. He swore to tell the truth, the whole truth, and nothing but the truth. However, I knew to expect lies, more lies, and nothing but lies.

Francisco's lawyer began the questioning process. While listening to the long-winded nonsense and lies from the lying guide, I followed Don's instructions and whispered to Colette, "He's lying and we have proof on file."

During Francisco's entire direct examination, I didn't stop whispering to her over and again, "He's lying and we have proof on file."

She totally ignored me. Once again, I thought, I'm dying.

Next came Francisco's cross examination. My corrupted lawyer did not ask any questions that required a yes or no answer. In fact, he allowed him the freedom of speech to talk up a lengthy storm of untrue rubbish. More wasted time. My lawyer's line of questioning definitely favored Francisco.

The lies continued until Don said, "I have no further questions."

To say the least, I was fuming. The entire session was orchestrated to waste time, so rebuttals would not be an option.

The sleepy magistrate closed the day's hearing by saying, "Both sides did very well."

Yeah, right. What a joke. How out of reality and into bull nonsense was the judge's comment?

He further stated, "The verdict will be in the mail shortly."

In my estimation, there was no need to wait for the verdict. I knew the outcome, because Francisco had two lawyers defending him, while I had two liars defeating me. Anyone with half a brain cell witnessing the proceedings would agree that such staging totally benefitted the defendant and totally shut down the plaintiff.

The defense team marched out of the trial room first. The three of them (Francisco, his lawyer, and **that lady**) had smiles from ear to ear. I didn't want to see the faces of Don and Colette. Those two dishonest traitors probably had that facial expression as well. I rushed out of the courtroom with so much anger and proceeded out of the building to the dirtiest car in Jersey, while the duo lingered behind.

Note: My lawyer's compensation (from **that** wealthy **lady**) due to Francisco's victory, would probably be coming shortly, just like the magistrate had said about the verdict, "It should be in the mail shortly."
End of note.

The evening was dim and chilly. Within a few minutes, the lying team arrived at curbside.

I told Don, "Hand me my phone. I'm taking a taxi to the hotel, also send me the entire file and Francisco's to my home, as you promised to do so." Don insisted on taking me to the hotel, but I refused.

He handed me my phone, together with a business card, which included his home phone number, and said, "If you want to talk, call me."

I really didn't want any more lies from the corrupt attorney, but I took my phone and his card.
Fast forward: Later on, Don's home phone number came in handy.
End of fast forward

Again, Don insisted that he'd take me back to the hotel, however this time I just ignored him.

The venomous paralegal opened her contaminated mouth and uttered, "Screw you, Conny, why are you resisting your lawyer's goodwill?"

That's her lingo, garbage produced more trash. Replying to such filth is not my way of handling any issues, so ignoring her was best during those tense moments. I then called for a taxi.

Agitation would not escape me as I entered the hotel. In the lobby, a complimentary plate of fresh fruit was offered to the guests. Since I had no appetite for dinner,

I helped myself to an apple and a banana. That's enough food for my body in turmoil. Needless to say, it was an awful, difficult, disturbing, and a very disappointing day.

To date, I wonder if the sleepy magistrate thought that I was a complete idiot for traveling over 2,000 miles to sue Francisco and having two lawyers defeat me.

On the other hand, the chief yawned constantly, therefore he probably had no idea what mostly went on in his court room.

Midnight approached and sleep was essential, but it would not come easy in my blistery state of mind. Instead of counting sheep, I counted the times I wanted to die during the ugliest and longest day of my life. The count was more than I bargained for.

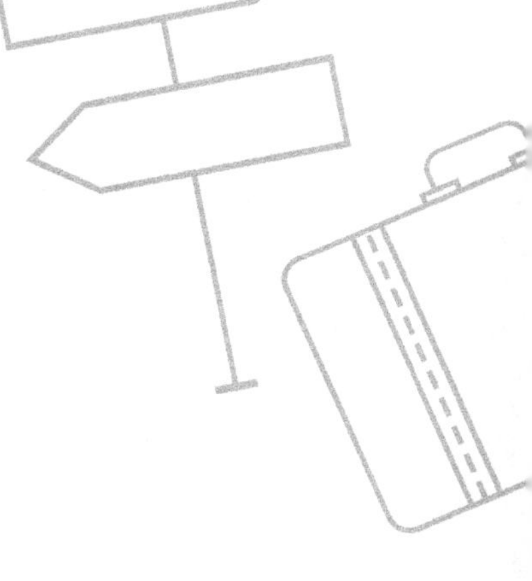

CHAPTER 49

Flying towards Better Days

I DIDN'T SLEEP A WINK. Gee, I wonder why? So, in the wee hours of the morning, I started to organize my belongings for the next journey, which would surely lead me to happier days and occasions.

Thoughts of visiting Israel eased my sad and disappointed mind.

The priority was getting to the airport ASAP. Breakfast could wait after I'd check in at El-Al's ticket counter and go through security, then I'll have my first meal of the day.

I hoped never to step in the state where I was unmercifully conned, so out the door and down I went to settle my room account, not forgetting to pay the hotel manager my heartiest compliments regarding the wonderful and professional staff.

I hopped on the shuttle for the ride to John F. Kennedy Airport. All went well as anticipated.

After replenishing my empty tummy, I had a three-hour wait for the long flight to Tel Aviv. Close to boarding, I needed a visit to the ladies' room. While washing my hands, I saw a black purse next to the sink. I thought, Uh-oh, someone's heart is racing. I waited a while for the person who left it, but the owner didn't show up. The only honorable undertaking was bringing it to security. On my way out of the ladies' room, a young lady rushed in, almost out of breath and all wound up.

She was so relieved when I asked her, "Is this yours?"

Her excited response was, "Oh, yes, thank God, and thank you!"

I replied, "I know the feeling."

Coincidentally, the lucky lady was on the same flight as me. When we crossed paths during the 11 hours in the air, she couldn't thank me enough. I shared with her the experience of forgetting my own purse. We both agreed to be more careful in the future.

Luckily, the seat next to me was empty. Therefore, I was able to stretch for some hours of sleep. After all, the day before had been my personal D-Day, and it followed a sleepless night.

The flight was smooth, likewise, the landing. I always praised the Israeli pilots, in my opinion they are the cream of the crop. Tearfully, I said shalom to the country that I'll always call my first home.

Going through customs and immigration, I realized that in less than 24 hours, I'd be attending Vivi's happy event, making the extra effort to join the wedding of her daughter was a given, and I couldn't be happier to do so.

My favorite cousin, Moshe, waited for me at the arrival lobby. I was invited to stay at his flat in Jerusalem, my favorite city. Upon entering Israel's capital city, I went into an emotional mode because I was born there just a month after Israel was declared an independent nation.

We arrived at what would be my home base for the next seven days. By the time I took a hot shower and settled into the guest room, which faced the famous King David Hotel, amazing Moshe went to a local falafel stand and surprised me with my favorite street food. How delicious it was.

After devouring my treat, I excused myself for a short nap. Did I have jetlag? Oh, yeah, it started three days ago, when I landed in New Jersey.

Some hours later and after a deep hibernation, my body stirred awake. It was the best sleep I had in recent memory. I felt completely rejuvenated and finally gaining energy for the upcoming event in a few hours.

Cousin Moshe insisted on driving me to Tel Aviv for the wedding. At first, I rejected the offer because the drive would be out of his way.

He persuaded me otherwise by saying, "I am going to visit Rachel (Moshe's sister, another cousin). She lives close to the banquet hall."

Only then, I agreed to accept the lengthy ride. I don't like to inconvenience anyone.

The wedding ceremony and reception were worth all the effort of traveling halfway around the world, however, the best was on its way, when I'll reunite with the rest of my family at Shabbat Eve dinner.

That night, Doron (another awesome cousin and Moshe's brother) hosted a beautiful dinner. Most of the family attended. All of us caught up with each other's good news since our last reunion. We then sang Shabbat melodies and the luscious food prepared by Aviva (Doron's wife) was second to none.

While in Israel, I learned that wonderful Pete and not-so-wonderful Kiti had split up. Pete moved to Tel Aviv permanently. I suppose that his goal was to be far as possible from the cat (smart guy).

I emailed him and suggested we meet for lunch. He replied and the get-together was scheduled. We met in Abu Gosh, a popular Arab-Israeli village nestled in the Judea Mountains (near Jerusalem). It's known for having the most famous and delicious Hummus.

The two of us had so much to talk about and we covered many subjects.

He shared with me various unpleasant incidents that took place during and post trip. Nothing surprised me with some of the hoodlums.

Pete is definitely a person to be trusted, therefore, I felt most comfortable with him.

Regarding the trial, his only comment was, "Your chances are grim."

Well, that was no news to me.

While wrapping up our reunion, Pete and I promised to keep in touch. We departed with a big hug.

After a week of tranquility and uplifting days in the land of milk and honey, to my first home, once again I said, "Shalom."

Unfortunately, the next time I heard about Pete, he had passed away, and I was sad.

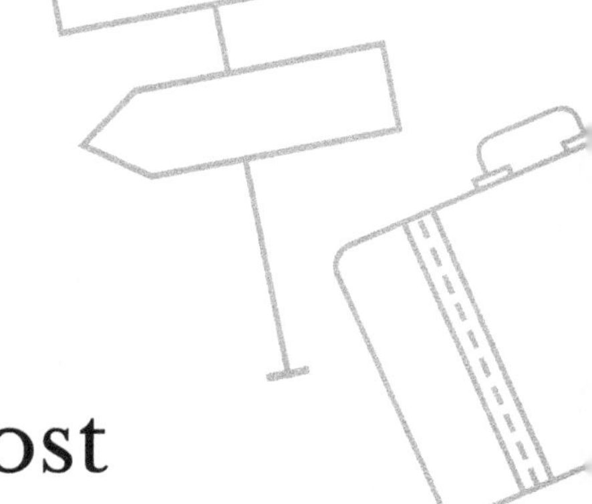

CHAPTER 50

First and Foremost

BACK HOME AND ON TOP of my mail stack appeared an envelope from the New Jersey court administration. It's a given that I lost and opening the envelope would be a waste of time and energy, but I was curious about Francisco's counter suit, so I opened it. Expecting the worst, I was right. Of course, I lost thanks to my lying and starving lawyer. However, there was a pleasant surprise! The sleepy magistrate did not award Francisco's reimbursement for his airfare to South America in the amount of $1,980. That was a small relief in the face of my huge and unjust loss.

I then thoroughly reviewed the magistrate's limited notes, it clearly stated that he based his verdict mainly on the agreement between me and Francisco. I was very surprised that the only two sentences which Francisco allowed me to input in the agreement, suggested extortion. That should have tipped the scale towards my victory.

To the best of my knowledge, extortion is illegal, and Francisco definitely extorted me.

Reminder: I'll quote said two sentences: "Francisco is demanding that Conny sign this agreement and cash the $400 check, only then, she will recover her needlepoint." End of reminder.

I had no choice but wait for my court files, then I'd have concrete details about the judge's decision. The package from Don's office should come any day.

The next item on the to-do list was reporting the incoherent judge. Of course, it would be another uphill battle and a long shot. The magistrate should have stayed home resting in bed because his body motion and lack of interest in my case meant he had health issues. Constant yawning on the job is not appropriate, especially in a court of law.

The only witness was Clarence (the court's clerk), and he is probably biased towards the court.

Regardless, I decided to go ahead with my complaint; miracles do happen from time to time. I called the courthouse with the purpose of speaking to Clarence. A long wait would have been no problem, I was prepared to hold until speaking to him. When his voice mail picked up, I left a message. No sooner than later, he promptly called me back.

After a detailed explanation regarding the nature of my call, I asked Clarence if he remembered the magistrate's rather poor participation throughout the entire trial and the eye contact between us immediately after my lawyer's outburst form his chair as I attempted to ask the magistrate a question.

The clerk answered, "I very well remember your case, however, I do not recall the eye contact between us regarding the magistrate's performance, I have no comments."

Clarence did admit remembering my case 'very well' (it was so recent, only nine days ago since my appearance at court), so how could he not recall the magistrate's lack of interest during the whole day and Don's rage jumping out of his chair to answer a question that was aimed to the judge? I didn't believe the clerk, but I got it. He would not defy his superior and risk a great job.

I'll never regret trying. Try is one of my favorite verbs.

CHAPTER 51

Unthinkable Solution

So FAR, I DID NOT receive the package as Don agreed and promised. The disloyal attorney committed to send it via my FedEx account, so when I'd return from the extended trip, all files will be at my home waiting for me.

After two weeks, nothing arrived from the state of New Jersey. I had a feeling this would happen.

Weathering the next storm meant calling the lying lawyer, so I did. My requests to speak with Don were met with responses such as: He's out to lunch. He's in a meeting. He's in court. He's sitting with a client. He's on the phone. Or I was just ignored. This went on for weeks. It was obvious that the excuses were bull nonsense and furthest from the truth. Don probably realized that by now I was well aware of his foul play.

The next month was a shaky roller-coaster ride. Many more attempts were made to get a hold of Don. I called, faxed, and emailed weekly, no response. One day, I finally reached him at 5:30p.m. his time. I suppose he was alone in the office.

From the abundance of crucial questions, I chose the obvious one, "Why are you not sending my court files as you agreed and promised."

He replied, "Give me some three weeks to assemble your file."

Then silence.

Note: In three weeks it would be four months since the trial and the promise to send me all court files.
End of note.

I couldn't believe what I just heard.

Before my next question, he announced, "It's after hours. I'll speak to you another time." The call was terminated. There were no other options for me to do, so wait I did.

The next bombshell came sooner rather than later. I received a letter from Don's office. Eagerly, I opened it only to learn that it was an invoice with a balance of $6,075! I was shocked. I knew that there would be a small balance due. However, this huge amount caught me off guard. His itemized services included three different meetings with Francisco's lawyer, each date exceeded more than an hour. It was another shock, because the invoice confirmed that Don actually admitted to be in default by spending hours with the defendant or his team. Our contract specifically stated that there would be no communications whatsoever between the two parties, aside from exchange of discovery, which does not take a long time to do. All this had to be a breach of contract!

Reminder: Don never shared with me a single item that he received from Francisco's attorney, whenever I asked about the defendant's evidence, I was told, "Don't worry, Conny. I have everything under control."
End of reminder.

My greatest fear was, if I didn't pay the dishonest lawyer, he could ruin my excellent credit and hold my files hostage (just like Francisco held my needlepoint).

During our next conversation, I told Don, "According to your invoice, you spent more than three hours with the defendant and probably his team. It was wrong, as well as illegal, because in our contract, it stated that you'll spend no time, aside for exchange of discovery with the defense team." Don did not have an answer.

I further said "Financially, I don't have the ability to pay you this huge amount." It's a mitzvah ('good deed' in Hebrew), lying to a liar (my opinion).

So, Don said, "Send me as much as you can."

The fact remained that he wasn't worth another red cent, but the worries that he'd tarnish my credit score was like a dark cloud hanging over me. I followed his directions and mailed the money-hungry unlawful lawyer two checks of $500, dated a month apart. The memo line read, 'Final Payment' thinking and hoping he'd send my court package. After all, he did say, "Send me as much as you can." I set the matter aside and waited for a response.

The following week, I received the checks back with a notation stating, "I do not agree to this amount."
Important Note: Being a lawyer, Don knew (and I did not) the following:

1. Keeping my court documents from me is illegal.
2. l had a four-month window to open a motion against him.

End of note.

Don chanced on the fact that I was not aware of those two options, he was right.

About two weeks dragged on and my court files were nowhere in sight, though I continuously called Don's office regarding their whereabouts. I had no success whatsoever.

One fine afternoon, I received a phone call from Don, he said, "I'll give you a huge discount, I'm willing to reduce your outstanding balance from $6,075 to $4,000 or offer me a fair settlement."

I answered, "I'll let you know in a few days."

I was beside myself and didn't want to tell the crooked lawyer how I really felt about him, because my files were still in his possession and I wanted my credit score left alone. Agitating him was not the solution.

My husband told me to settle with him on his offer.

I replied, "Over my dead body."

Meanwhile, the days turned into four months.

Most nights, I couldn't sleep a wink, déjà vu from the sleepless hours after Francisco's trial. While thinking what could be done regarding Don's lawless behavior, my mind shifted to an unthinkable idea. I finally came to terms that what had to be done will be done.

The following morning, I called the New Jersey small claims courthouse and opened a second case, this time against the nefarious Don. Yes, my ex-lawyer.

I happened to speak with a very nice senior clerk, Nancy. I told her every detail about Don's performance during my case against Francisco and his refusal to send my court files. The clerk seemed shocked, but I realized that an employee of the court could not share any opinion.

Instead, she said, "Before I help you with the lawsuit against your ex-lawyer, you have the right to open a motion against him."

I asked her what that meant, she explained, "A motion is a request for a Judge to make a decision on a given issue pertaining to a trial which has already been decided."

My reply, "I wish I'd known that before, let's open it now."

The kind clerk looked up my case against Francisco and gave it a quick read.

Sighing heavily, she said, "Mrs. Connors, your option to open a motion expired two days ago. It exceeded the four-month margin."

Only then, I understood why Don is keeping my files for the duration of four months.

At this point, I was very frustrated. Don had wormed his way out of facing a motion and conning me at my trial against Francisco. He had gotten away with two major actions.

I proceeded with the lawsuit against my former attorney. Within 48 hours, Don would be served.

Note: To open a lawsuit there has to be a monetary demand and seeking my court files bears no stated financial value, so I went for the maximum $6,000. I expected nothing, but hoped for the return of my entire court file and a zero-dollar balance to my deceiving lawyer.

End of Note.

As much as I didn't want to set foot in New Jersey, I'd have to put my feelings aside and face this state again.

Don was served to appear at his trial in six weeks.

Days later, I finally received the court files from Don's law firm. Now that I have my files, and the verdict was final, having a case against Don would not be necessary. There was nothing more for me to pursue.

I called the courthouse. While speaking to the same clerk, Nancy, I told her, "I'm dropping my case." A minute later she said, "Mrs. Connors you cannot drop the case."

Shocked, I asked, "Why not?"

She replied, "Your defendant, Don, is countersuing you for the maximum amount of $6,000. The paperwork is in the mail, you should have it in a few days."

That bombshell was devastating, but I'd deal with it later. For the time being, I could finally review the contents of my files.

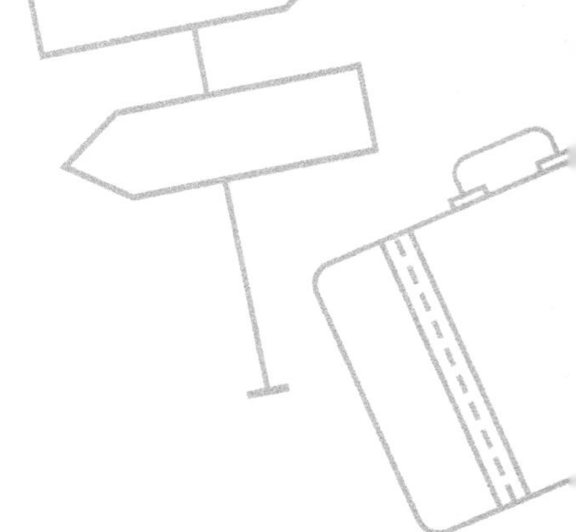

CHAPTER 52

What a Joke

WHILE TAKING A HUGE BREATH, I opened the box from Don's office. Oh, my God! Whoever had the chore of assembling my package just dumped all the papers in. It looked like they'd been hit by a hurricane. Nothing was in chronological order, neither paper clips nor staples were in sight. No civil pattern of organization was exercised and the negative energy from inside the package spilled out.

The first item that popped into my hands was a letter to the New Jersey's small claims court. It was handwritten in poor penmanship, as if a child wrote it. Its contents displayed promoting Francisco's leadership and demoting me. The signature was Hell-en's.

Reminder: Did this royal moron forget that she was the first one to announce loud and clear, "No tip for Francisco from me!" Said quote was delivered while waiting for Francisco and his extremely late bus transfer to the parade.

Regarding Hell-en's corrupted mind and filthy mouth, there is no adjective strong enough to describe this beast's character.

End of reminder.

A good friend of mine named Bella (she knows the notorious Hell-en), told me the following, "Hellen is denying that she wrote a complaint letter against you."

I then showed my friend the letter that Hellen had indeed wrote to the court. Bella was speechless. Did I mention that Hell-en is a pathological liar, as well as her other negative characteristics.

I then began to organize the mess from the East Coast. Papers were all around here, there, and everywhere.

After the tedious job of organizing the files, it was easier to review them.

I found what I was looking for, it was the 'list of exhibits,' it's a one-page sheet that lists the body of evidence from both parties. Conny's list (the plaintiff) to the left side of the sheet in numerical order and Francisco's list (the defendant) to the right side in alphabetical order.
The items listed as evidence in my section were as follows:

1. The travel agency's registration
2. My travel agent's certification
3. A letter of recommendation from my employer, over 25 years ago
4. Another letter of recommendation from 30 years ago
5. A complimentary letter from a couple on the doomed trip
6. Another complementary letter from the same trip
7. A brochure from the cruise line
8. Another brochure from Brazil's tourist office
9. A photograph of my needlepoint
10. A group photograph taken at the Iguazu Falls
11. A map of South America

I was beyond mortified, all of the 11 pieces from the evidence were the nonsense that Don asked me to send him because of his fake story that I didn't have enough proof. I wouldn't have believed it if I hadn't seen the defected exhibit list with my own eyes. All of the strong evidence that created hefty weight on my case had not passed through the doors of the courthouse.

Missing 11 pieces, the most vital evidence that should've been on the list of exhibits were:

- The detailed letter from Maritza
  She testified all about the impossible tour that went terribly wrong in São Paulo, as a result it escalated into a dangerous situation.
- Maritza's contract and itinerary
  She'd received them from her boss, Jose.
- My contract and itinerary
  Delivered to me from Francisco,
  The immediate above two documents differed from each other, they should have been exactly the same.
- Maritza's business card,
  She'd written, "Conflicting contracts! Conny's itinerary is impossible to do in one day!" She signed and dated it.
- A letter from the Israeli lawyer
  She explained in full detail about the very dangerous transfer to the ruined parade viewing.
- My canceled check payable to Shlomo
  This satisfied his demand for the returned tip that he gave Francisco.

- A joint letter from three couples
  They requested their tip money back from Francisco.
- The agreement between me and Francisco
  It bore the two sentences suggesting extortion regarding my needlepoint, I'll quote, "Francisco is demanding that Conny sign this agreement and cash $400 check. Only then will she recover her needlepoint."
- A copy of the $400 check
  Had I not cashed it, Francisco stated in the agreement that I would not see my needlepoint again, it suggested extortion.
- A copy of the complaint letter from the family of four
  They'd written to the New Jersey Attorney General, complaining about Francisco's very poor services during their vacation in Uruguay.
- The packet of legal precedent (previous similar cases)
  It had been prepared by Paula, the pregnant attorney.
  Note: Don's opinion of the immediate above was "Money well spent."

End of my silent evidence.

I was floored. All of my strongest proof that should have been presented to the court had been illegally stored away by my own attorney.

How sad that after many hours on the phone with my lawyer explaining each piece of evidence, I still chose to fly thousands of miles so we could verbally go over my entire file. The end result, not one single piece of my extremely vital proof was presented to the court. Flying to the east coast did nothing for my case. Now I understand why Don told me, "No need to fly over 2,000 miles, I have everything under control."

The items listed as evidence in Francisco's section were as follows:

A. Map of Rio's stadium
B. A picture of the group
C. Payment receipt
D. Another payment receipt
E. Airline tickets
F. Receipt for airfare
G. Photo from Iguazu Falls (Argentina's side)
H. Photo from Iguazu Falls (Brazil's side)
I. Hell-en's letter

Note: The next four pieces of evidence are disturbing. My lawyer had kept them from me because three were totally fabricated, thus, illegal.
End of note.

J. A letter, via email

Supposedly it was sent from Jose, the Santos-based tour company's manager.

After reading every word carefully, I realized that it was full of lies and wild accusations.

The letter went on blaming, accusing, and painting a terrible picture of me. A thought crossed my mind: Perhaps Francisco had written this letter. I tested my theory by sending an anonymous email to the sender pretending I'm a new customer seeking information about São Paulo. Sure enough, I was right. The reply came from the crooked guide and not Jose. It was simple, Francisco wrote the letter to himself while posing to be the manager of the tour agency in Santos, Brazil. So, in actuality, the letter was a fraudulent piece of evidence presented to the court.

K. Another letter, via regular mail

Again, supposedly from Bernardo, the manager of the Iguazu Falls National Park in Brazil.

The contents were similar to 'exhibit J,' complaints about me. This letter contained a phone/fax number and mailing address. I called, faxed, and wrote to supposedly Bernardo, but all communications went unanswered. My gut feeling suggested that this was another fraudulent letter. After all, there is definitely a pattern of Francisco writing to himself pretending to be someone else.
Another fraudulent document to the court.

L. An invoice of $1,500 from Francisco's lawyer.

It was specifically addressed to a female's name (this couldn't be anyone else but **that lady**). Said document proved that she, (**that lady**) was sponsoring Francisco's legal expenses.

M. A very crucial and fabricated document was an altered agreement between Francisco and me.

Obviously, Francisco or his defense team deleted my two sentences, which Francisco only allowed me to input in the original agreement and then a rewritten agreement, minus my two sentences was presented to the court. I'll repeat the two deleted sentences: "Francisco is demanding that Conny sign this agreement and cash the $400 check. Only then, she will recover her needlepoint." Another fraudulent document to the court.

The Fabricated (Rewritten) Agreement

Written below is a copy of the rewritten agreement.

"This is an agreement between Conny Connors and Francisco.

After all the services provided to Conny by Francisco in South America, including Buenos Aires, Iguazu Falls, Montevideo, Punta del Este, Rio de Janeiro, and São Paulo, Conny had 2 complaints. One of the complaints was with the tour bus in São Paulo and the second complaint was with one of the transfers in Rio de Janeiro, Brazil.

Even though the full amount was paid to the bus companies and we agreed that once paid, the funds were non refundable which the proof of the non refundable condition is signed and initialed by Conny and Francisco, as proof.

Francisco is offering a refund of $400 to Conny, in a form of a check, per good customer service. Francisco is also sending Conny's needlepoint.

After this agreement is signed by both parties, Francisco is mailing the needlepoint to Conny and no further claims will be done. This means no money claims from neither party."

X Conny did not sign
Signature

X Francisco signed and dated
Signature

Note:

1. The original agreement possessed six paragraphs, in the fifth paragraph it stated: "Francisco is demanding that Conny sign this agreement and cash the $400 check. Only then, she will recover her needlepoint."
2. Francisco and/or the defense team deleted the statement above from the original agreement, which surely indicates an illegal document was presented to the court.
3. The tired magistrate failed to notice that my signature and date were missing in the fraudulently rewritten agreement.
4. Only Francisco signed and dated this fabricated agreement.

Note: I believe that Don did not inspect the documents of whoever put my package together. Had he reviewed the outgoing docs, I'm sure he'd never have allowed exhibits 'J' through 'M' to end up in my hands.
End of Note.

An important reminder: In the magistrate's verdict, he clearly noted that his decision was mainly based on the agreement between Francisco and me. Since the original agreement was definitely rewritten (tampered with) then presented to the court, it's nothing but a fraudulent document. If this wasn't enough corruption, the tired magistrate failed to notice that my signature and date were missing. Only Francisco's signature and date appeared on the illegal (rewritten) agreement. How honest of the defense team not forging my signature.
End of reminder.

The verdict was clearly incorrect. A perfect recipe for Francisco to prevail, and me to fail. If that was not immoral and unjust, I don't know what is. More bad news, no appeal to be granted in smalls claims court. Needless to say, I was extremely disappointed and shocked.

Don did a wonderful job sabotaging my case, no wonder his infamous quotation was, "Conny, don't worry. I have everything under control." Really, what my lawyer controlled was Francisco's path to victory (of course, with the generous help of the wealthy female friend, **that lady**).

To date I wonder the amount he received from her. How in the world could I have the slightest chance of prevailing on my case that had so much evidence towards winning?

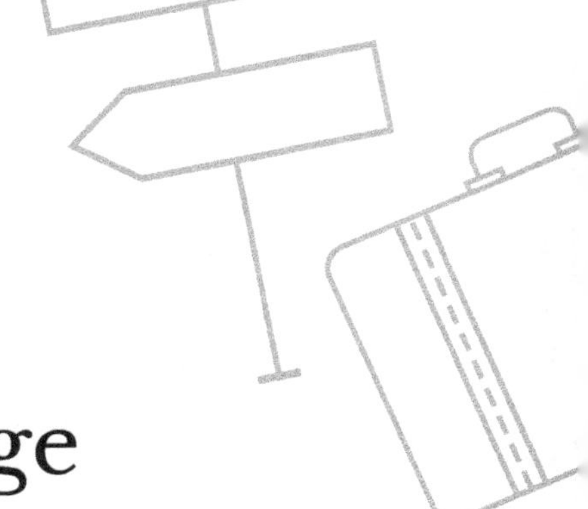

CHAPTER 53

On a Greater Edge

The court date of Don's countersuit against me slowly approached. I had a reason why I lagged in making my airline and hotel reservations. The hesitation came from knowing that I would see the dishonest lawyer who was compensated to fail me by Francisco's rich female friend.

I resigned myself to the reality that I'd have no choice other than facing the unethical, barbaric lawyer again, so traveling some 2,000 miles to appear in court was a must. In the event I don't show up, I'd automatically lose and have a mandate to pay Don an additional $6,000. This amount would be on top of the nearly $5,000 I'd already paid him, plus the monetary reward (of an unknown sum) paid to Don by **that lady** for his success in shattering my case against Francisco. That's a lot of money for a lot of corruption.

Reluctantly, I made my flight and hotel reservations (one night only). I was already waiting to be back home from the would-be hellish rendezvous I'd undergo in New Jersey.

A week before the trial, and while reading a local newspaper, I saw a few pages of wanted ads. One ad in particular was a familiar name. An Israeli lawyer had an advertisement offering a free half-hour consultation. What could

I lose? If anything, I'd gain a 30-minute assessment about Don's cockamamie countersuit. I called the law office and made an appointment. The wait was not too long and within a couple of days I sat in front of the young attorney. His physical attractiveness was undermined by a nervous demeanor. I briefed him with the important details and bizarre behaviors regarding my experiences with Don.

I carefully listened to his feedback as he told me, "Mrs. Connors, your ex-lawyer will chew you up in his home state, allow me to propose a settlement between the two of you. My fee will be $1,250."

I answered, "I'll think about it and thank you for your precious time."

I thought, yeah right, another hungry lawyer that needs to be fed. Instead of elevating my low feelings about the countersuit, he suppressed them further down.

Don should've been disbarred for purposely failing me on my case. I wanted to tear his law license in pieces and throw it into the nearest body of water. I wished and prayed that justice would be found, not only in the dictionary, but also in the state where I was royally conned.

Days later, I took an early-morning flight and landed in the late evening. After a short cab ride, I soon checked in at the hotel. That night, I had a terrible time falling asleep. My mind was racing with thoughts of what could happen in court the next day. After all, being sued by a lawyer in his home state, versus a nervous female out of state and not with a law degree, will be another uphill battle. Regardless, I reviewed my testimony for the following day.

While still awake in bed and having heavy thoughts, I came to the conclusion that Don's countersuit was unusual and the only thing to do – is tell the truth, the whole truth, and nothing but the truth. I also made a decision to keep a positive attitude. From then on, that small change of mind made a big difference in my frame of thinking and it allowed me to unwind for some solid sleep.

Waking up at dawn with a growling empty stomach wasn't a surprise. I had very little to eat for nearly 24 hours, so breakfast was the priority before diving into the unknown and nerve-racking day. I didn't forget the episode of leaving my handbag at the hotel's restaurant, so for a second go-around, I held it tightly to prevent the same from happening again. Live and learn.

Today's courthouse was in a different town than the first trial. This one seemed to be in an upscale area with lots of greenery. The weather was favorable while I walked to the court's address, a mere mile from the hotel. I arrived on time. Sitting alone in the lobby, I waited until the door opened for my designated hearing room and hoped that Don would not show up, but the one who had conned me eventually arrived. Yes, my heart raced to its capacity.

No sooner than later, he approached me and had the chutzpah to ask, "Conny, can we settle our case out of court?"

I answered, "Oh sure! All you need to do is pay me double the amount that you were paid by **that lady** in your illegal bribe to fail me and prevail Francisco. You defended the defendant and not me, the plaintiff, your honest paying client."

Don didn't dispute my accusations, he just answered, "See you inside."

I refrained myself from telling him, "Inside jail is where you belong!"

Within a few minutes, we entered the courtroom and were sworn in. My testimony detailed the many experiences that I had with Don's unlawful and unprofessional actions. Of course, he didn't like to hear the truthful statements. My ex-lawyer objected to practically every one of them. I was shocked when he opposed to the fact that he specifically instructed me multiple times, "Conny on your direct examination you are to answer yes and no only, on cross examination look at my facial expression then you'll know immediately to stop talking." Yet here in court, he denied those dramatic instructions and everything else relating to the truth.

Next came Don's turn on the stand. I just couldn't believe my ears. The lies and nonsense that came out of his mouth, floored me.

The worst part was when he outright said, "Your Honor, Mrs. Connors' entire testimony is a lie."

Once again, we were informed that the verdict would be sent via US mail. The day ended in ample time to catch my flight without any stress.

My opinion about the judge was as follows:

- He gave his undivided attention to the presentations by both sides.
- Took notes
- Was wide awake

His interest in the case seemed to be balanced and fair, unlike the worn-out magistrate from the previous trial.

I quickly walked out of the courthouse avoiding my nemesis and took a taxi to the airport. I made it through security easily and then onto the plane. While flying back home, I remembered the commitment that I vowed to stay positive. My heart was set on not expecting any refund from the hungry and unfaithful attorney, however I hoped the judge wouldn't award Don $6,000 from me.

Arriving back home and starting the wait for my wonderful mailman Robert to deliver the nerve-agitating verdict.

When the envelope from the court arrived, my pulse was on a marathon. First and foremost, I needed to sit down preventing a fall on the cold marble floor. The last thing needed was a broken bone on top of a broken heart, if I lost.

With squinted eyes and taking yet another deep breath, I opened the envelope and read the verdict that had been rendered. It stated, "Mrs. Connors' case is not within the criteria of this forum. A Grievance Committee is the proper arena to find a solution."

Don's countersuit, dismissed.

Hallelujah a million times. Finally, something positive from the state that brought me so much grief. Thankfully, the judge was wide awake and did not believe any of Don's nonsense. My ex-lawyer can only dream in his deepest sleep to receive an additional $6,000 from me.

I wanted to know all about the grievance committee which the court recommended. I learned that it would put together a three-member panel, two liars—Uh-Oh! Sorry I mean, two lawyers—and one businessperson. They were to determine the case and the majority would prevail. This option is valid up to four months (a familiar time frame). The worst scenario popped into my mind, could **that lady** possibly wiggle her way to any or all three members by swaying them with her wealth? Just a ridiculous thought.

Frankly, I had huge issues with the rather small state to say the least. I deserved a big time out from all the legalities. Defeating Don was a triumph, but it took a toll on me. Regarding the Grievance Committee, I'll attend to it at a later time.

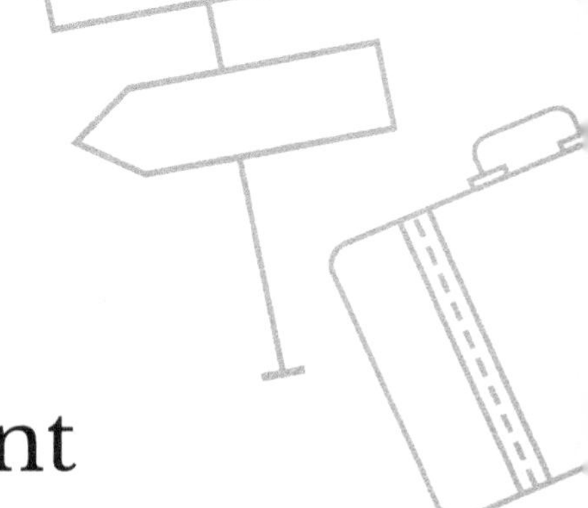

CHAPTER 54

Money Well Spent

Though I prevailed in the strained second trial, I still weathered stress from the lies and illegal activities that Don caused me. It had indeed stretched my nerves to the limit.

Now that this whole episode came to an end, my husband was adamant about taking a short getaway hoping rejuvenation and rest would help to heal my shattered nerves.

Five days in Kauai was the prescription. It didn't take long to make reservations, but with a twist, I made sure that the entire trip did not exceed $6,000, in order to commemorate my winning against a lying lawyer in his home state.

The day before our trip, while making some last-minute calls regarding the mini vacation, I pressed a wrong key on my cell phone.

After a few rings, I was told, "Hold on, please."

Wow! I recognized the voice. It was Don's paralegal Colette. Apparently, she also made a mistake by not placing the call on mute, therefore, I was able to hear most of what was happening in the office. Don's thunderous rampage must have been heard up and down the East Coast. It sounded so loud, as though he was having a meltdown (without mercy) on some poor individual. Such extreme hysteria would impact anyone's blood pressure through the roof.

I could somehow put together the blasting screaming words which were associated with Don's loss in his countersuit against me. I froze with the phone against my ear and it had me trembling. Something was totally out of the norm.

Within seconds, Colette, the paralegal said, "May I help you?" I simply terminated the call.

The next day, Alex and I were up and on our way to relaxation and unwinding, which I desperately needed.

We flew some six-and-a-half hours over the Pacific Ocean and happily arrived at our destination. The greetings of leis assembled with beautiful orchids and a friendly aloha were most welcoming after the long flight.

Kauai was just wonderful as my husband had predicted. Most of the time was spent taking long walks, doing some water sports, and dining out. I immersed myself in the flourishing tropical atmosphere, resting did both of us a world of good. This getaway was, to quote Don's famous line, "money well spent."

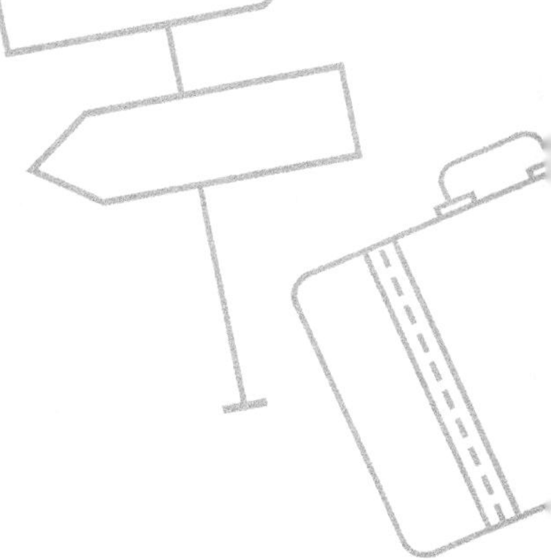

CHAPTER 55

In Disbelief

Back home after the Hawaiian trip, I couldn't help but think about my mistaken call to Don's office.

I had no idea what prompted me to call again, but I did (which is out of my character).

After a few rings a recording answered and played the following message, "This law office is no longer in operation, pending cases will be addressed soon. We apologize for any inconvenience."

Stunned again and shaken, I hung up the phone. It had only been six days since I'd overheard Don's raging voice in the middle of his meltdown. I wondered what happened.

Quickly going into my files to dig up Don's home phone number, I located his business card.

Curious Conny dialed, I recognized his wife Michelle's voice and politely said, "Hello ma'am, my name is Cathy, I'm looking for Attorney Don, he was referred to me as I'm in search of a lawyer in his specialty, would it be possible to leave him a message?"

Her voice cracked with sadness as she answered, "My husband had so much stress in his law office, it caused him to have a massive heart attack. He died six days ago."

In the second of silence that followed, I recalled Don's scary screaming hysteria from the week prior, regarding losing his case against me. In disbelief, I gave her my condolences and said goodbye.

After a simple calculation, I came to the conclusion that Don must have passed away the same day I called his office by mistake.

CHAPTER 56

A Worthwhile Session

UTTERLY MIXED FEELINGS WENT THROUGH my mind. After the many unethical and illegal actions that Don performed on my case, I wished for his disbarment from practicing law. Most everyone in my situation would feel the same. However, a death sentence did not sit well with me.

My adrenaline went haywire. It was hard to digest what Michelle had just told me regarding stress over my case and causing her husband's final fate.

Any attorney defeated in their home state by a non-savvy law person from out of state, would've been devasted, furthermore, their reputation and pride would surely suffer.

For Don's sake, I believe he should have never filed a countersuit against me and just have the case drop. I also strongly believe that if Don had indeed let the case free, his law office would still be open, thus sparing his life which is much more than $6,000.

Another theory of mine was, if **that** wealthy **lady** had not been so involved in my case, Don would have represented me ethically and legally. I had all the tools to prevail, but my lawyer couldn't resist the temptation of more money coming in.

At times, being greedy has a short lifespan.

It didn't take a genius to realize that my case against Francisco was presented to the court in the worst and illegal manner. It took a gutsy, dumb lawyer rejecting an easy win. Unfortunately, it was hard for Don to refuse a bribe. In actuality, **that lady's** wealth lead to Don's senseless decision of accepting a bribe.

Because I was carrying such a heavy load and needed emotional support from an objective entity, I searched for a reputable psychologist. After choosing one that felt like a good fit, an appointment was scheduled.

What a relief to have a few sessions sorting out the issues during the doomed trip and thereafter. The evaluations that I gained on all complicated matters helped me in all directions. It was worth every dollar and hour spent.

The late Don's famous quote applied again: "money well spent."

As we concluded the last session, and said our goodbyes, the therapist quipped, "By the way, Mrs. Connors, you should think about writing a book, it would be interesting, informative, educational, and entertaining."

I agreed, and added, "There's a lesson to be learned, being greedy is not the **way**, it took Don's life without further **delay**."

AFTERWORD

Years later, I learned the following:

Due to the late Don's malpractice with one of his cases while still practicing law, a lean against his family's estate was in progress.

Justice should have succeeded, but in Don's world, money superseded.

Printed in the USA
CPSIA information can be obtained
at www.ICGtesting.com
LVHW091123310124
770455LV00001B/80